Days

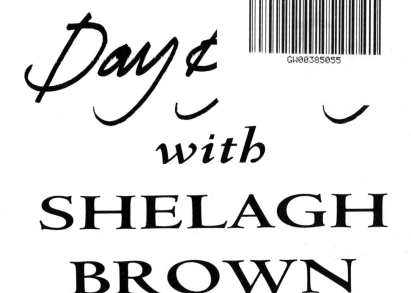

with

SHELAGH
BROWN

Day by Day

with

SHELAGH BROWN

Bible readings and
prayers for every day

Copyright © 1998 The Bible Reading Fellowship

Published by
The Bible Reading Fellowship
Peter's Way
Sandy Lane West
Oxford
OX4 5HG
ISBN 0 7459 3502 8

First edition 1998

10 9 8 7 6 5 4 3 2 1 0

Acknowledgments
Good News Bible copyright © American Bible Society 1966, 1971,
1976, 1992, published by the Bible Societies and
HarperCollins*Publishers*.
The Jerusalem Bible copyright © 1966, 1967 and 1968 by Darton,
Longman & Todd Ltd and Doubleday & Company, Inc.
The New Jerusalem Bible copyright © 1985 by Darton, Longman &
Todd Ltd and Doubleday & Company, Inc.
The Revised Standard Version of the Bible, copyright © 1946, 1952, 1971
by the Division of Christian Education of the National Council of
the Churches of Christ in the USA.
The New Revised Standard Version of the Bible copyright © 1989 by the
Division of Christian Education of the National Council of the
Churches of Christ in the USA.
The Holy Bible, New International Version, copyright © 1973, 1978,
1984 by International Bible Society/Hodder & Stoughton Ltd.
New English Bible copyright © 1970 by permission of Oxford and
Cambridge University Presses.
Revised English Bible copyright © 1989 by permission of Oxford and
Cambridge University Presses.
Material from *The Alternative Service Book 1980* is copyright ©
The Central Board of Finance of the Church of England and is
reproduced by permission.
Hymn 'O Breath of Life' copyright © the Estate of Elizabeth
Porter Head.
The Lion, the Witch and the Wardrobe and *The Magician's Nephew* by C.S.
Lewis, published by HarperCollins*Publishers* Ltd.
Lent for Busy People edited by Shelagh Brown copyright © 1993 BRF.

A catalogue record for this book is available
from the British Library

Printed and bound in Slovenia by Sloprint

CONTENTS

*This book is dedicated
to the memory of Shelagh Brown
by her colleagues at
the Bible Reading Fellowship:
Shelagh was a dear friend to many of us
as well as an ebullient colleague.
Her vision and writings were an inspiration
while she was with us,
and we pray that many more people
will continue to find
similar inspiration in this book.
The Bible Reading Fellowship
will make a donation to* **TEARF**UND
*for every copy sold of
Day by Day with Shelagh Brown.*

Introduction

On 29 June 1997 the Church of England lost probably its best-known woman priest, the Bible Reading Fellowship an outstanding Editor, and thousands of people all over the world a valued friend and counsellor. The accident at home that cost Shelagh Brown her life left many people, who had never actually met her, feeling bereaved. So the hope is that this book, a compilation of some of her best devotional writing on the Bible, will go some way, at least, to filling the gap she has left.

Shelagh Brown grew up in a traditional church setting, with a faith that she later felt was second-hand, at best. It was when she was living and working in London that that faith came alive, largely through the ministry of the famous All Souls' Church, Langham Place. There she met Christ in a new and dynamic way, an experience that remained with her all through the rest of her life, as an inspiration and as a daily reminder of the power of God to change people's lives.

One important effect of that experience was to introduce Shelagh for the first time to the Bible as a living book, a book that could influence her daily life. Someone told her that Christians should read the Bible 'every day', regularly and expectantly; so she did. She came to it, in her own words, like a starving beggar who has found bread. She read it at every imaginable opportunity, without plan or discipline, but with irresistible enthusiasm. 'I simply couldn't get enough of it,' she said. Out of that burning hunger for the word of God grew a lifelong commitment to reading the Bible, and sharing its riches with others.

When she entered Christian ministry, initially as a deaconess, the Bible was her constant companion and inspiration. It was the basis of her preaching and teaching, her praying, and her pastoral concern. Without holding a narrow or literalist view of the text, she nevertheless lived her life by its teaching and shaped her beliefs and her behaviour by the 'Word of God written'. Shelagh truly was a 'woman of the Book'.

Her ministry as a deaconess, and then as a deacon, is remembered with affection and appreciation by many people. Shelagh was a born communicator—indeed, Archbishop Coggan chose her to lead his Training Services Centre, with its emphasis on Christian communications skills. Yet, in a wonderful way, the best for her was yet to come.

It was her appointment to the staff of the Bible Reading Fellowship in 1991, and especially as Editor of *New Daylight*, that brought a new and fertile field for her gifts—and she was now in her sixties. Her subsequent ordination as priest seemed to give her a further injection of energy and inspiration, so that ideas, articles and books seemed to flow from her in an endless stream—not all of the ideas, to be honest, strictly practical!

Her greatest gift was to make the text of the Bible come alive—to take the sacred words of prophets and apostles and apply them to the lives of her readers, just as she had applied them to her own life for so long. Sometimes she achieved this by means of a fitting, real-life illustration—a child at the tea-table, the builders working outside her house. Above all, she had an uncanny insight into how her readers *felt*. You were aware of a person who really did share their lives, anxieties and hopes.

This selection draws from her writings for *New Daylight* over a period of several years, and ranges far and wide across the scriptures she loved so much. The style is unmistakable, the faith infectious, the enthusiasm utterly genuine. It is a book to warm the heart and to strengthen faith—'day by day'.

David Winter

The
WISDOM
of
GOD

To teach me obedience

In the days of his flesh, Jesus offered up prayers and supplications, with loud cries and tears, to the one who was able to save him from death, and he was heard because of his reverent submission. Although he was a Son, he learned obedience through what he suffered; and having been made perfect, he became the source of eternal salvation for all who obey him, having been designated by God a high priest according to the order of Melchizedek.

Obedience is not a fashionable quality these days—except for dogs. Zach, the beautiful alsatian who lives in the stables next door to my house, is properly obedient. His owner is wonderful with creatures. They love her and they obey her. Zach pads along with the horses when they go down to the heath—close to heel when he is told to be, and coming back from interesting rabbit thickets when he is called.

On the other hand, the sheepdog down the road (who used to live in Scotland and couldn't cope with our traffic) was a menace to all the local cars. He chased them—probably thinking they were a special sort of sheep which he had to bring to order. So he had to go to obedience classes. Now when he hears a car he crouches on the ground until the sound of the engine has died away in the distance. He has learned obedience, and it is safer for him and safer for us.

The obedience that Zach the alsatian gives to his mistress comes from the relationship between them. It isn't a cowed obedience. He wants to please her. And at a far, far higher level it is that sort of obedience that we give to God. The obedience of a love relationship. Not that God speaks to us like a bad father—'Do as I say or I will box your ears!' But he tells us what the right way is for us—and then wants us to trust him, even if it hurts. Deuteronomy 8:2–5 tells of the way God led the Israelites:

The test

Remember the long way that the Lord your God has led you these forty years in the wilderness, in order to humble you, testing you to know what was in your heart, whether or not you would keep his commandments... Know then in your heart that as a parent disciplines a child so the Lord your God disciplines you.

Just listen!

When Job's three friends, Eliphaz of Teman, Bildad of Shuah, and Zophar of Naamah, heard of all these calamities which had overtaken him, they set out from their homes, arranging to go and condole with him and comfort him. But when they first saw him from a distance, they did not recognize him; they wept aloud, tore their cloaks, and tossed dust into the air over their heads. For seven days and seven nights they sat beside him on the ground, and none of them spoke a word to him, for they saw that his suffering was very great.

When we are in deep distress and feeling very sad, another person's presence can be a real comfort to us. On the whole it is better if they don't say anything to us, but sit in silence. If we can bear to sit with someone like this, there is a sense in which we are bearing their pain with them. Not taking it away, but entering into it. With *compassion*—which is to 'suffer with'.

It is costly and painful to sit like that in silence—and Job's friends did pretty well to stick it out for so long. The pity was that they ever started talking as they did. But most people cannot bear the helplessness of not being able to help—of not being able to solve the problem.

Two friends of mine lost their eldest son in a car accident. They were devastated, and in deep distress, and some of their Christian friends couldn't endure their pain. So they tried to talk them out of it. 'Where is your Christianity in all this?' one person asked the mother. It made matters worse and didn't help at all—and the bereaved parents withdrew themselves into a protective shell. If their friends understood so little and caused them so much hurt, then they didn't want to see them.

Reflect

Try to remember a time in your life when you have felt desolate and hopeless. Did anything or anyone ease your distress? In someone else's distress, could you sit in silence and refrain from giving advice or prodding them to perk up and remember their Christian faith? Reflect on the words of Paul: 'Weep with those who weep,' he wrote to the church at Rome. Not, 'Stop crying and blow your nose and cheer up.'

You are... you will be

Simon Peter said to him, 'Lord, where are you going?' Jesus answered, 'Where I am going, you cannot follow me now, but you will follow afterward.' Peter said to him, 'Lord, why can I not follow you now? I will lay down my life for you.' Jesus answered, 'Will you lay down your life for me? Very truly, I tell you, before the cock crows, you will have denied me three times.'

A small girl I know isn't very good at knowing her own limitations. She loves her food, and when she sees one of her favourite dishes on the table she demands a big helping. One day when she had come to lunch her face gleamed with pleasure at the prospect of roast lamb, roast potatoes and peas. But when she saw the size of the helping I had put on her plate she scowled. 'More!' she said. 'No,' I said. 'You won't finish it. You can have some more when you've finished this.' 'No—now!' she said, getting cross. So I gave her what she insisted she could eat, and warned her that if she didn't finish it she wouldn't have any ice-cream and butterscotch sauce afterwards. Afterwards arrived, and we sat there for a long time while other people ate their ice-cream and she refused to eat the rest of her roast potatoes. It had a fairly happy ending—with concessions made on both sides.

Like Peter, my young friend didn't know herself very well. Peter thought he could manage more than he could for the sake of Jesus. But Jesus knew just what Peter could and couldn't manage. 'You are Simon...' Jesus said. 'You will be called Cephas' (which means rock). Dr Campbell Morgan says that Jesus knows what he can do with Peter. He can take the little rock that he is—the shifting, shaley sand of human nature—and transform it into Petros, the divine nature. Perhaps there is an echo of that in 2 Peter 1:3 and 4: 'His divine power has given us everything needed... He has given us... his precious and very great promises, so that through them you may... become participants of the divine nature...'

A prayer

Lord Jesus, help me to know my limitations, and also to know you. By your divine power (and because you love me) may I share your divine nature. Amen.

Cry out for me!

My child, if you accept my words and treasure up my commandments within you,
making your ear attentive to wisdom and inclining your heart to understanding; if
you indeed cry out for insight, and raise your voice for understanding; if you seek it
like silver, and search for it as for hidden treasures—then you will understand the
fear of the Lord and find the knowledge of God. For the Lord gives wisdom; from his
mouth come knowledge and understanding; he stores up sound wisdom for the upright;
he is a shield to those who walk blamelessly, guarding the paths of justice and preserv-
ing the way of his faithful ones. Then you will understand righteousness and justice
and equity, every good path...

In chapter 1 of Proverbs, Wisdom cries out for us to listen to her. Here she
is telling us to cry out to her. Wisdom is like a relationship. It doesn't land
on our laps full grown and ready made. It starts small, like a seed taking
root—and we know that we want to grow the plant because we have seen
it growing in other places and in other people, and it attracts us. On tele-
vision once, I saw a man who had a passion for fuchsias; and he had
travelled to the heights of the Himalayas to search for unknown species of
the plant that he loved. When we set out on that sort of search for wisdom
the promise is that we shall certainly find it. But unless we really desire it
we shall never set out. When God is speaking to the Jewish exiles in
Babylon through the prophet Jeremiah this is what he says:

'I know the plans I have for you,' says the Lord, 'plans for your welfare
and not for harm, to give you a future with hope. Then when you call
upon me and come and pray to me, I will hear you. When you search for
me, you will find me; if you seek me with all your heart' (Jeremiah
29:11–13).

A way to pray

Spend a few moments reflecting on your own life... and then on the national life of
your own country. Reflect on the tragic stupidity and folly of so many people. Will
you commit yourself to search for wisdom, so that God can bless you and other people
through you?

Wise and foolish

'Every one then who hears these words of mine and does them will be like a wise man who built his house upon the rock; and the rain fell, and the floods came, and the winds blew and beat upon that house, but it did not fall, because it had been founded on the rock. And every one who hears these words of mine and does not do them will be like a foolish man who built his house upon the sand; and the rain fell, and the floods came, and the winds blew and beat against that house, and it fell; and great was the fall of it.' And when Jesus finished these sayings, the crowds were astonished at his teaching, for he taught them as one who had authority, and not as their scribes.

As I write, the man next door, Charlie, is digging the foundation for his new house. He has three other men and a mechanical digger to help him, and the foundations are being cut over a metre deep and half a metre wide into the clay soil. Then tomorrow thirty tons of concrete will be poured into the trenches to make a rock-like foundation for the new, and quite small, house to stand on. When it is built the strong west winds that blow in our part of the country will never be able to shift it.

But what are the winds that might blow us over—if we don't have our foundation on the rock that is the teaching of Jesus?

Perhaps they are the winds of God that will test our lives on the last day, when all that we have made of the house of our life will stand in the presence of the God who is wind and fire, and who has committed the judgment to the man Christ Jesus.

The Sermon on the Mount sums up all of Christ's teaching. It can change our whole world if we follow it. But we shall only be able to follow the teaching if we follow the Teacher.

The Lamb upon the throne

And between the throne and the four living creatures and among the elders, I saw a Lamb standing, as though it had been slain... and he went and took the scroll from the right hand of him who was seated on the throne. And when he had taken the scroll, the four living creatures and the twenty-four elders fell down before the Lamb, each holding a harp, and with golden bowls full of incense, which are the prayers of the saints; and they sang a new song, saying, 'Worthy art thou to take the scroll and to open its seals, for thou wast slain and by thy blood didst ransom men for God from every tribe and tongue and people and nation, and hast made them a kingdom and priests to our God, and they shall reign on earth.'

When we hear the story of the first Easter morning, we listen to the glorious words which tell us about the resurrection of Jesus Christ from the dead—and the joy and bewilderment and disbelief of those first disciples. But the resurrection of Christ happened once in time—and the appearances and the empty tomb were events experienced and seen by the ones who were there in the beginning. For us the present reality is not that Jesus rises again from the dead every Easter but that he rose on that first Easter morning.

It was the risen Christ whom John saw in the series of visions which form the book of Revelation. Earlier in this vision John has been weeping, because he has seen a scroll sealed with seven seals containing God's future plans for the earth, and no one has been found worthy to open the scroll. But John is told not to weep, because 'the Lion of the tribe of Judah, the Root of David, has conquered' so he can open the scroll. Yet when John looks he sees a Lamb. The purposes of God can go forward, but only because the Lamb has been slain and Christ has died for the sin of the world...

A song of praise

Forever You will be
The Lamb upon the throne
I gladly bow the knee
And worship You alone.

Noel and Tricia Richards

The gift of God

For by grace you have been saved through faith, and this is not your own doing; it is the gift of God—not the result of works, so that no one may boast. For we are what he has made us, created in Christ Jesus for good works, which God prepared before-hand to be our way of life.

Once I had an unpleasant and unhappy argument with a very learned theologian. 'God will save everyone,' he insisted. 'But what if they don't want to be saved?' I asked. That was several years ago, and I have since learnt more sense. Arguing is fairly futile, and the theologian began to get irritated with me. 'You are saying it depends on us,' he said, 'but it all depends on God.' 'Yes,' I agreed, 'of course it does—in one sense. We cannot save ourselves. But surely we have to *receive* forgiveness and accept the love of God?'

You can't *make* somebody love you. They have to respond to your love. For me it is like the empty hands that I hold out at Communion—to be given the body and the blood of Christ. The greatest theologians in the world have argued about this issue, and Augustine and Pelagius wrangled on for years. Paul is quite clear that our salvation isn't our own doing—it is the gift of God. Gifts, though, have to be received—if we want them. We then have to use them for the purpose for which they were created. God has made us to do good works—and that doesn't mean going round patronizing people. It means loving them, and the way to know what *that* means is to work out how we would want to be treated in their circumstances. Some decisions are easy to make. If we are hungry and thirsty, we want another person to feed us and give us something to drink. Sometimes, though, we don't know what the right thing to do is, or what the 'good' action is. We can pray then for wisdom—confident that God will give it to us.

Pray

Pray for an end to futile arguments in the Church. Then think of a particular need you know—and pray for the wisdom to work out how to meet it.

A precious stone

Come to him, to that living stone, rejected by men but in God's sight chosen and precious; and like living stones be yourselves built into a spiritual house, to be a holy priesthood, to offer spiritual sacrifices acceptable to God through Jesus Christ. For it stands in scripture: 'Behold, I am laying in Zion a stone, a cornerstone chosen and precious, and he who believes in him will not be put to shame.' To you therefore who believe, he is precious, but for those who do not believe, 'The very stone which the builders rejected has become the head of the corner,' and 'A stone that will make men stumble, a rock that will make them fall': for they stumble because they disobey the word, as they were destined to do.

Next door they were building a house and the work suddenly slowed down. So I went to see why. The builders told me they were getting the corners right. If they don't, the house will start to lean like the tower of Pisa. So the quoin at the corner of each line of bricks is the crucial brick. In an arch it is the stone in the middle that takes all the thrust of the sides and holds them together. That is what Jesus is for Zion.

Once upon a time there was a city divided by walls into four parts. In one part all the people and animals and houses were red, in another green, in another blue and in another yellow. All the people thought their colour was the best and they never spoke to each other. But one morning the red people found a great black stone in their midst. They painted it red, but the paint wouldn't stick. So one night they threw it over the wall to the green people—and the green people threw it over to the blue—and the blue to the yellow. The stone wouldn't change. It stayed obstinately and beautifully black. But the people started to change. They climbed up their walls and started to talk about the problem of the stone. And they enjoyed talking, so they started to knock down the walls. Then they used the bricks to build a church, within a great fourfold arch, at the centre of the new city. And the cornerstone of the arch was the great black stone.

Now we can understand

With all wisdom and insight he has made known to us the mystery of his will, accord-
ing to his good pleasure that he set forth in Christ, as a plan for the fulness of time, to
gather up all things in him, things in heaven and things on earth. In Christ we have
also obtained an inheritance, having been destined according to the purpose of him who
accomplishes all things according to his counsel and will, so that we, who were the first
to set our hope on Christ, might live for the praise of his glory. In him you also, when
you had heard the word of truth, the gospel of your salvation, and had believed in
him, were marked with the seal of the promised Holy Spirit; this is the pledge of our
inheritance toward redemption as God's own people, to the praise of his glory.

Yesterday I read a novel by Dick Francis, the best-selling author who was
the Queen Mother's jockey and who now writes superb mysteries about
the world of racing. He understands people and he understands horses—
and he has helped me to understand what I never had before: the relationship between a horse and its rider. I would never have understood the
mystery unless Dick Francis had written about it.

It is like that with the mystery of the will of God. He reveals it to us so
that we can understand and appreciate it. The Communion service itself
would be a total mystery and a closed book to someone who didn't know
the story of Jesus. But once we know that story, we can understand. 'Take,
eat, this is my body which is for you...' And through *that* story we can
understand the will of God for his world—a plan almost beyond belief: 'To
gather up all things in him, things in heaven and things on earth.' We are
all part of the plan whether we choose to be or not. Everything will be
gathered up, including us, whether we choose it or not. But we can
choose to be part of the glory, and to be a child of God through the grace
of God. Then we are sealed with the Spirit—a mark that we belong to God,
and a down-payment on our future glory.

A way to pray

Reflect on the mystery of the will of God—made known now through Jesus Christ.
Reflect on the glory you know now—and on the glory that you will know.

The man who is God

For to us a child is born, to us a son is given, and the government will be on his shoulders. And he will be called Wonderful Counsellor, Mighty God, Everlasting Father, Prince of Peace. Of the increase of his government and peace there will be no end.

I wonder if Isaiah had to do the sort of intellectual anguishing that theologians have done ever since the birth of Jesus, wrestling with the question of how it is possible to be 'truly God and truly man'. I think it is only as we worship that we can know the truth and the glory of it. 'By love may He be gotten and holden, but by thought never,' wrote the unknown author of *The Cloud of Unknowing*, and that is just as true of the mystery of God the Son.

The Counsellor has all the wisdom in the world—because he was there in the beginning when the worlds were made. In Proverbs 8:30–31, Wisdom says, 'Then I was the craftsman at his side. I was filled with delight day after day, rejoicing always in his presence, rejoicing in his whole world and delighting in mankind.' That one is *our* counsellor, so if we have problems we can be fairly confident when we ask for help! The Counsellor is also the mighty God—so in our weakness we can know his strength, and do what we could never do on our own—love our enemies, do something effective for the hungry and the homeless, tell the good news to a sad, bad world. The child who is born is also the everlasting Father—and although there are three 'Persons' in the Godhead, God is 'One'. He is the Holy One of Israel, and the God of the whole earth, and when the child who was born grew up he said, 'I and my Father are one.'

A reflection

Think of the Son of Man and the Son of God being born as a baby in Bethlehem, where there was no room in the inn. See it in your mind's eye... Then spend some time reflecting on the names and the nature of the baby who is the Son: Wonderful Counsellor... the Mighty God... the Everlasting Father... the Prince of Peace. Then worship him.

Matthew 24:37–42 (RSV)

He will come again

As were the days of Noah, so will be the coming of the Son of man. For as in those days before the flood they were eating and drinking, marrying and giving in marriage, until the day when Noah entered the ark, and they did not know until the flood came and swept them all away, so will be the coming of the Son of man. Then two men will be in the field; one is taken and one is left. Two women will be grinding at the mill; one is taken and one is left. Watch therefore, for you do not know on what day your Lord is coming.

When life gets too much for her, a friend of mine says hopefully, 'Wouldn't it be lovely if the Lord would come again!' She was brought up in a church and in a generation for which the Second Coming was a lively part of their belief, and they would examine the signs of the times to see if the fig tree was bursting into leaf and they might shortly expect the arrival of 'the Son of Man coming in clouds with great power and glory' (Mark 13:26). Then the troubles of this life and 'the elect' (which of course included them!) would be with God for ever in the glories of heaven.

But whatever those mysterious words mean (and Jesus seems to have said them several times) they are not about a magic deliverance from our present difficulties and distresses. It is right in the middle of these things that we can know the presence of the living God and be given the wisdom of Christ to know what to do. But one day our earth will come to an end. The Bible and science both agree on that. One day you will die (and one day I shall) and on that day Jesus will do for us what he told his disciples he would do for them: 'I will come again and will take you to myself, that where I am you may be also' (John 14:3). Not the Second Coming at the final end of the world—but a coming for us at our final end. In the meantime we have work to do in the sad and sinful world which God created and loves and died for. We have to tell it the good news of the love and forgiveness of God-in-Christ, to feed its hungry, clothe its naked, and provide homes for its homeless. So pray to know how to redeem the time (as the Bible puts it) which you have between now and the coming of Christ for you.

John 16:4b–7 (GNB)

The helper

I did not tell you these things at the beginning, for I was with you. But now I am going to him who sent me, yet none of you asks me where I am going. And now that I have told you, your hearts are full of sadness. But I am telling you the truth: it is better for you that I go away, because if I do not go, the Helper will not come to you. But if I do go away, then I will send him to you.

It was an astonishing thing for Jesus to say—and the disciples (not for the first time) were slow to understand. 'It is better for you that I go away.' How could it be? They loved him and needed him. They had followed him since the start of his ministry, and for three years he had taught them and told them about God the Father as no one had ever done before. But then no one ever could have done—because this was God the Son, unique in all the world. Imagine what it was like for them to live in the presence of the Son of God, and learn from him, and spend all their days with him, and eat all their meals with him.

'Better for you that I go away...' How could it be? It was his presence that was so wonderful—and that's what they wanted, not his absence. And it was his presence they were going to have, in a way that was even more wonderful than the last three years had been. Then his physical presence was there for them—if they were there with him. But if they weren't there then they couldn't enjoy his presence and they couldn't go on discovering about God from his teaching. And if they needed his help they couldn't have it—if he wasn't there. But in the future they *would* have his help, and his presence. Not his physical presence, but his spiritual presence. And not outside them, but inside them.

The Spirit of Jesus would come and live in their hearts—and in all our hearts right down to the present day, if we will receive him. When you go to Holy Communion, and eat the bread that is the body of Christ, and drink the wine that is the blood of Christ, realize afresh that Christ is in you—God with us—Emmanuel. Not outside you. Inside you—like the bread and the wine. God the Holy Spirit. The Counsellor, the Comforter and the Helper. There for you—and, through you, for the world that he made and loves and longs for.

So be deeply thankful—and admit that what Jesus said to his disciples was true—for them and for us. 'I am telling you the truth: it is better for you that I go away, because if I do not go the Helper will not come to you.'

Don't worry . . .

'And why are you anxious about clothing? Consider the lilies of the field, how they grow; they neither toil nor spin; yet I tell you, even Solomon in all his glory was not arrayed like one of these. But is God so clothes the grass of the field, which today is alive and tomorrow is thrown into the oven, will he not much more clothe you, O men of little faith? Therefore do not be anxious, saying, "What shall we eat?" or "What shall we drink?" or "What shall we wear?" For the Gentiles seek all these things; and your heavenly Father knows that you need them all. But seek first his kingdom and his righteousness, and all these things shall be yours as well. Therefore do not be anxious about tomorrow, for tomorrow will be anxious for itself. Let the day's own trouble be sufficient for the day.'

If we worry, there is something wrong with our relationship with God. And since none of us ever gets that right all the time then we are going to worry for some of the time.

But we need to look at whatever we are worrying about and examine it, as it were, in the presence of God, and tell him all about it.

Then we must listen—because there will be an answer. Today's passage is part of the answer.

Another part might be, 'You eat too much, my child—or drink too much—or have quite enough clothes and don't need any more—and what about my children who haven't got food or clothes or houses or medical supplies?' It might be, 'Cut up your credit card and throw it away.' It might be, 'Don't let the world around you squeeze you into its own mould.'

Reflection and prayer

Read the passage again—slowly and prayerfully—and ask God to speak to you through it.

His delight

*The Lord created me at the beginning of his work, the first of his acts of old. Ages ago
I was set up, at the first, before the beginning of the earth. When there were no depths
I was brought forth, when there were no springs abounding with water. Before the
mountains had been shaped, before the hills, I was brought forth; before he had made
the earth with its fields, or the first of the dust of the world. When he established the
heavens, I was there... when he marked out the foundations of the earth, then I was
beside him, like a master workman; and I was daily his delight, rejoicing before him
always, rejoicing in his inhabited world and delighting in the sons of men.*

This passage is about wisdom, whom the Jews wrote about as a person.
They said (not in the scriptures, but in other writings) that before the
foundation of the world God dandled two children on his knees—his wisdom and his word. The revelation of God that was given to the Jews was
incomplete, but it was very deep. They knew that God was personal, and
that he loved the human race. Their understanding of God was that a
mighty energy went out from him like a word, to create all that is—and
that all that is was created with wisdom.

Just as God was a person, so wisdom and the word were also personal,
rejoicing over the world and delighting in the people who lived in it. Do
you realize that the God who created you actually delights in you?

A meditation

*Think of the galaxies spinning round on their orbits in space... Think of this
earth—and the sun and the moon. Think of a blackbird... a dolphin... a seal...
and other living creatures. Think about a person whom you love... and then think
about yourself, and be aware of yourself—sitting on your chair, or perhaps sitting up
in your bed. Think of the wisdom that made all these things... of the energy of the
word that made them... and of the personal, loving God, who made you and me and
all that is, delighting in his world and his creatures.*

Don't hit back!

For to this you have been called, because Christ also suffered for you, leaving you an example, that you should follow in his steps. He committed no sin; no guile was found on his lips. When he was reviled, he did not revile in return; when he suffered, he did not threaten; but he trusted to him who judges justly. He himself bore our sins in his body on the tree, that we might die to sin and live to righteousness. By his wounds you have been healed. For you were straying like sheep, but have now returned to the Shepherd and Guardian of your souls.

Humanly speaking it is an impossible standard we have been set—and without the Spirit of Christ within us it would be impossible to contemplate it. The world answers back and fights back when it is attacked. We are told not to—because Jesus didn't. When I am driving and an aggressive driver tries to cut me up by passing me on the wrong side, my natural reaction is either to accelerate and stop him getting in, so that he squeals to a stop, or if he happens to manage it then I give a long sustained hoot. Not always, but more often than I should. The Spirit of Christ is having a battle with me about it—and only sometimes winning it. But I am convinced of the rightness of the theory, even if I only sometimes put it into practice.

Living as Christ lived is to let the evil come to a halt in our own body. It is to take it into ourselves and not to hit back. Christ took all the evil of the whole world into his own body on the tree—so that we might stop sinning and hating and start living and loving. Really living. Really loving. He was wounded. We are healed because of it. We were lost like sheep. Now the shepherd has found us and rescued us. But it cost him all he had.

A prayer

Lord Jesus Christ, help me more and more to see the glory and the wonder of the way you lived. Help me not to fight back when people (and drivers) annoy me. Help me to accept their evil and let it stop in me—so that it doesn't go any further. Give me your Spirit to be my helper, day by day.

How to get it right

If any of you lacks wisdom, he should pray to God, who will give it to him; because God gives generously and graciously to all. But when you pray, you must believe and not doubt at all. Whoever doubts is like a wave in the sea that is driven and blown about by the wind. A person like that, unable to make up his mind and undecided in all he does, must not think that he will receive anything from the Lord.

What James says about asking for wisdom follows directly on from saying that Christians' response to the test of their faith should be joy (see James 1:2–4). But if they don't know how to get it right then they are to ask God to give them wisdom. 'Now this thing has happened to me—how can I use it in the right way, so that I grow through it?' is the way to ask. Wisdom is about knowing the way really to live one's life. 'Blessed is the man who finds wisdom, and the man who gets understanding,' it says in Proverbs (3:13). 'Her ways are ways of pleasantness, and all her paths are peace. She is a tree of life to those who lay hold of her; those who hold her fast are called happy. The Lord by wisdom founded the earth' (Proverbs 3:17–19). James says that the God who is the source of all wisdom will give it to us if we ask. But when we ask we mustn't doubt. God loves to give to us, and he is a generous giver. He gives a measure that is filled up and running over, like the measure that Jesus talked about in the Gospels. And when he gives us wisdom he is giving us nothing less than himself—to be with us in the suffering. It is Christ himself who is both 'the power of God and the wisdom of God' (1 Corinthians 1:24), and what we need in our trials isn't just a set of instructions on how to behave but a person to be with us in the depths of our being and the depths of our pain.

A prayer

Lord Jesus Christ—give me wisdom—and give me yourself.

In everything God

We know that in everything God works for good with those who love him, who are
called according to his purpose. For those whom he foreknew he also predestined to be
conformed to the image of his Son, in order that he might be the first-born among
many brethren. And those whom he predestined he also called; and those whom he
called he also justified; and those whom he justified he also glorified.

What Paul says here is the most sublime statement of faith about our suffering that has ever been made. 'In *everything* God works for good with
those who love him', or 'in *all* things God works for the good of those who
love him...' If we lose our job or our money, if we fail our examination, if
our husband or wife walks out on us, if the person we love doesn't marry
us, or if we get put into prison (Paul was put there, and so was Joseph back
in the Old Testament)—we know that all those things God works for our
good. And what is true in our suffering is also true in our happiness and
in our successes—a happy marriage, a satisfying job, a business that flour-
ishes. In all things and everything God works for good. He can use every
single thing that happens to us to conform us to the image of his Son.
That's what his purpose is—to make each one of us like Christ, all of us
shining with the glory of God. That is our ultimate good. And God will
work through all things to fulfil his good purpose for us.

A prayer

Lord God, it's hard to believe. That in all things you work for the good of those who
love you. I do love you, Lord—though often my actions don't match up to my love. I
remember now before you the things that I find hardest in my life—those things that I
find it hardest to believe that you can work through for my good... But Lord, I do
believe... Help thou my unbelief...

Beautiful new clothes

Awake, awake, put on your strength, O Zion; put on your beautiful garments, O Jerusalem, the holy city; for there shall no more come into you the uncircumcised and the unclean. Shake yourself from the dust, arise, O captive Jerusalem; loose the bonds from your neck, O captive daughter of Zion.

Israel has gone to sleep, and God is calling to her to wake up and get dressed. The people of God must wake up to who they are and put on the beautiful clothes that their God (and husband) will give to them (his bride).

Once I was in a shop watching a friend try on a beautiful bright yellow suit. She looked at herself in the mirror and smiled at her reflection. She had been feeling rather low, and new clothes can somehow lift our spirits up. An outward sign of leaving old things behind and making a new beginning. That is what God wants the people of God to do—and he buys the beautiful new clothes for us. We can think about the cost of them another time. Today we shall just look at the clothes.

The daughter of Zion has been sitting in the dust. So she is dirty. Added to that there is a fetter around her neck. Unclean and un-free she is, and also powerless in her own strength. But the beautiful clothes that God will give to her (if she will put them on) will give her God's strength. Then she will be able to break her fetters and be what she is meant to be. Clean— and free—and holy.

A meditation

Imagine a bride sitting in the dust with a fetter round her neck. Imagine the husband who loves her giving her new clothes and strength. Then imagine her, in her beautiful clothes, at an Easter Parade—showing off the beauty and the glory of God in a world spoilt with the ugliness of fear, hate and hopelessness. A world that might lift up its head and dare to hope as it looks at the beautiful Easter clothes of the people of God.

Pray for peace

First of all, then, I urge that supplications, prayers, intercessions, and thanksgivings be made for all men, for kings and all who are in high positions, that we may lead a quiet and peaceable life, godly and respectful in every way. This is good, and it is acceptable in the sight of God our Saviour, who desires all men to be saved and to come to the knowledge of the truth. For there is one God, and there is one mediator between God and men, the man Christ Jesus, who gave himself as a ransom for all, the testimony to which was borne at the proper time. For this I was appointed a preacher and apostle (I am telling the truth, I am not lying), a teacher of the Gentiles in faith and truth.

In the Roman Empire in which this letter to Timothy was written all the kings and rulers can't have been Christians. But Christians were to pray for all of them—and to pray for peace. And for the Jew and for the Christian, peace was far more than the absence of war or strife. Rather, it was the presence of all those things which make for humanity's highest good— right relationships between people and nations, social justice, and free- dom to sit under your own fig tree (which was about having your own place and your own space). These things only happened when the loving will and righteousness of God was lived out in a loving social system in which everyone mattered. Peace has to do with right and loving relation- ships between human beings—and between them and their God. Peace would only come into being through the reconciliation that Jesus Christ came to bring—through his birth, his life, his death and his resurrection, and then the giving of his Holy Spirit. 'Peace on earth, good will towards men…' through the Christ of God. So Christians were to pray for peace— and for their kings and rulers. There could be no peace on earth without the Prince of Peace—so the prayer of all Christians for all those in author- ity has to be that they will come to know the 'one mediator between God and man, the man Christ Jesus, who gave himself as a ransom for all'. God our Saviour wants 'all men to be saved and to come to the knowledge of the truth'. Our task is to pray for them so that they will.

The power of God

To keep me from becoming conceited because of these surpassingly great revelations,
there was given me a thorn in my flesh, a messenger of Satan, to torment me. Three
times I pleaded with the Lord to take it away from me. But he said to me, 'My grace
is sufficient for you, for my power is made perfect in weakness.' Therefore I will boast
all the more gladly about my weaknesses, so that Christ's power may rest on me.
That is why, for Christ's sake, I delight in weaknesses, in insults, in hardships, in
persecutions, in difficulties. For when I am weak, then I am strong.

The problem of a prayer that isn't answered is what we are looking at today. And it was an apostle who prayed it, pleading with God to give him what he wanted—and to take away what he didn't want. We don't know what it was, except that it hurt him and he didn't like it. But he doesn't tell us any more than that—and it is good that he doesn't. Because now we can apply what happened (and what didn't happen) to Paul to our own circumstances.

Paul prayed and pleaded and God didn't answer his prayer. Or that's what we might say. Yet 'No' is just as much an answer as 'Yes'. And God didn't leave it at a stark 'No'. He made Paul a promise. 'My grace is sufficient for you, for my power is made perfect in weakness.' Then Paul must have turned to a different sort of prayer—in which he opened himself up to the grace and the presence and the power of Christ. And God did what he promised—so much so that Paul then started to boast about his weaknesses and to delight in them.

Reflect

Is there something that you long for God to take away from you? Something you have
pleaded and prayed about and yet you are still stuck with? Could it be that God is
saying to you what he said to Paul? If it is possible, then start to pray differently.
Praise God for your weakness—and for his power. Then wait, expectantly, for his
power to be made perfect in your weakness.

The wisdom of God

My son, if you accept my words and store up my commands within you, turning your ear to wisdom and applying your heart to understanding, and if you call out for insight and cry aloud for understanding, and if you look for it as for silver and search for it as for hidden treasure, then you will understand the fear of the Lord and find the knowledge of God. For the Lord gives wisdom, and from his mouth come knowledge and understanding.

If we pray for wisdom, God will give it to us. 'If any of you lacks wisdom, let him ask of God, who gives to all men generously and without reproaching, and it will be given him. But let him ask in faith, with no doubting...' (James 1:5, 6). Wisdom isn't cleverness. It isn't about being intellectual and passing examinations. It is something far greater and deeper than that. It was through wisdom that God created the world, and later on, in Proverbs, Wisdom says that 'when he marked out the foundations of the earth, then I was beside him, like a master workman; and I was daily his delight, rejoicing before him always, rejoicing in his inhabited world and delighting in the sons of men' (Proverbs 8:29b–31). In the New Testament Christ is 'the power of God and the wisdom of God'—and we too can be given power and wisdom if we pray for it.

A way to pray

Think now of a situation in your life where you really need wisdom. Tell God about it (it can help to write things down) and ask him to give you wisdom. Don't doubt that he will... trust him. Spend a few moments just reflecting about the situation... and when you have an idea or thought, now or later, write that down and consider it. The wisdom that made the galaxies and field mice and poplar trees and people will be given to you for your need.

So that I can grow

Consider it pure joy, my brothers, whenever you face trials of many kinds, because you know that the testing of your faith develops perseverance. Perseverance must finish its work so that you may be mature and complete, not lacking anything. If any of you lacks wisdom, he should ask God, who gives generously to all without finding fault, and it will be given to him. But when he asks, he must believe and not doubt...

A woman was talking with me about a difficult relationship in her family. Her mother was unbelievably manipulative. She poured out a stream of presents (largely unwanted) on the whole family—and she always wanted her own way. She wanted to go on holidays with them and to be included in everything. When they confronted her with her behaviour she said they were making her ill—and managed to be ill! My own grandmother used to have an attack of angina every time anybody crossed her. She would collapse in a chair and take little swigs of the whisky she always carried round with her for this sort of occasion.

'Consider it pure joy... whenever you face trials... because you know that the testing of your faith develops perseverance.' For those of us at the receiving end of the testing, like the woman with the difficult mother, all that happens is an opportunity to develop our spiritual muscle and grow into mature human beings—a Christian 'not lacking anything'. There is no other way to do this growing than by being tested.

Pierre de Caussade used to say to his nuns, to whom he was spiritual director, 'You should be pleased that such tough things are happening to you—it is God's opportunity for you to grow!' We shall not grow if we opt out, or let the manipulative mother/brow-beating boss walk all over us. It won't be good for us or for them if we do. They need to be confronted—not fiercely, necessarily, but with the truth—and to know how to do that we need all the wisdom of God. And it is promised to us—if we ask.

A way to pray

Think of the situation in your life that is the greatest trial to you. First of all thank God for it. Then ask for wisdom to deal with it.

Because I am mortal

The days of our life are seventy years, or perhaps eighty, if we are strong; even then their span is only toil and trouble; they are soon gone, and we fly away. Who considers the power of your anger? Your wrath is as great as the fear that is due you. So teach us to count our days that we may gain a wise heart.

I have just been interrupted by a telephone call from a friend to say that a friend has died. He was 89 years old, and had a massive coronary after diving into a swimming pool. Last week I went to the funeral of a man aged 78 and the week before that of a man of 72. One of the answers to the question 'Why should this happen to me?' (or to him or her) is quite simply that this is the way the world is.

It seems as if it is good for us, in the present state of things, only to have a limited span of life. In the story of our beginnings in Genesis the logic of God driving Adam and Eve out of the Garden is that they are at risk there. If they stay they might eat the fruit of the tree of life and live for ever. But in the broken world that we live in, that would have been bad for them and for us. Dr Johnson said (I assume to Boswell), 'Depend upon it, Sir, when a man knows he is to be hanged in a fortnight, it concentrates his mind wonderfully.' And the fact that we know we shall not live for ever (even if we try not to think about it) has something of the same effect.

'Why should this happen to David?' a woman once said to me in anguish, when her husband died after many years of suffering. 'He was such a good person…' But being a Christian and being good (not that we ever totally are) doesn't mean either that we shan't die or that we shan't suffer. It simply means we ought to be able to handle it better.

Reflect

The only religious way to think of death is as part and parcel of life; to regard it, with the understanding and with the emotions, as the inviolable condition of life.

Thomas Mann, *The Magic Mountain*

Mind pictures✓

God speaks to us in dreams and in visions. When St John was in exile on the Isle of Patmos, God gave him a vision which was a revelation of Jesus Christ and of the things that were to come. It is a book filled with strange and wonderful symbols, and we don't always know what they mean. But if we see the pictures in our mind's eye—and really look at them—they will speak the truth of God deep into our hearts. They aren't meant for us to analyse with our intellects. Symbolism is about a far deeper level of communication than that. In chapter 19 John describes his vision of heaven:

And the twenty-four elders and the four living creatures fell down and worshipped God who is seated on the throne, saying, 'Amen. Hallelujah!' And from the throne came a voice crying, 'Praise our God, all you his servants, you who fear him, small and great.' Then I heard what seemed to be the voice of a great multitude, like the sound of many waters and like the sound of mighty thunderpeals, crying, 'Hallelujah! For the Lord our God the Almighty reigns. Let us rejoice and exult and give him the glory, for the marriage of the Lamb has come, and the Bride has made herself ready; it was granted to her to be clothed with fine linen, bright and pure'—for the fine linen is the righteous deeds of the saints. And the angel said to me, 'Write this: Blessed are those who are invited to the marriage supper of the Lamb.'

Christ is the Lamb whose marriage is about to happen, and his Bride is 'the holy city, new Jerusalem' (21:2), which is filled with 'the saints'—the holy ones, who belong to God, and who do holy things. They have 'washed their robes and made them white in the blood of the Lamb' (7:14), so they have 'the right to the tree of life and that they may enter the city by the gates' (22:14). But outside the city are 'the dogs and sorcerers and fornicators and murderers and idolaters, and every one who loves and practises falsehood' (22:15). Inside there will be those who did those unholy things in the past. But they won't have gone on doing them.

A meditation

Shut your eyes and think about John's vision of heaven. See it in your mind's eye, and let God speak to you through it.

Even when it's unjust . . .

Servants, be submissive to your masters with all respect, not only to the kind and gentle but also to the overbearing. For one is approved if, mindful of God, he endures pain while suffering unjustly. For what credit is it, if when you do wrong and are beaten for it you take it patiently? But if when you do right and suffer for it you take it patiently, you have God's approval.

This is one of the toughest passages in the New Testament—on a par with loving our enemies and doing good to those who hate us and despitefully use us, which Jesus told us to do in the Sermon on the Mount. In Rome slaves did all the work—including being teachers and doctors and musicians and actors. Sometimes the slaves were much-loved members of the family they worked in—but in law they had no status. A slave was just a thing, not a person. Slaves had no human rights because they were not regarded as human. They knew they were in their hearts. They were bound to, because every human being is made in the image and likeness of God. And now Christianity had told them that what they hardly dared to believe was true—that in Christ, 'There is neither Jew nor Greek, there is neither slave nor free, there is neither male nor female; for you are all one in Christ Jesus' (Galatians 3:28).

So now what? Were they to band together and revolt? They could have taken over Rome if they had. But Peter says, 'No'. Treat your masters with all respect—not just the kind ones but the cruel ones as well. Why? Because in Christ's passion and suffering the glory of God shone out into the darkness of the world with a brightness that had never been seen before—the glory of God in the face of Christ crucified. In their own small way that is what the slaves of Rome were called to do. In our even smaller way so are we.

A prayer

Lord Jesus Christ, teach me what it means to endure pain while suffering injustice. May I know the power of your resurrection and the fellowship of your suffering.

Only one master...

'No one can serve two masters; for either he will hate the one and love the other, or he will be devoted to the one and despise the other. You cannot serve God and mammon. Therefore I tell you, do not be anxious about your life, what you shall eat or what you shall drink, nor about your body, what you shall put on. Is not life more than food, and the body more than clothing? Look at the birds of the air: they neither sow nor reap nor gather into barns, and yet your heavenly Father feeds them. Are you not of more value than they? And which of you by being anxious can add one cubit to his span of life?'

The Aramaic word *mamon* simply used to mean material possessions. It comes from a word which means 'to entrust', and so *mamon* was the wealth which a man entrusted to someone to keep safe for him. But Barclay says that over the years it came to mean 'that in which a man puts his trust', and then *mamon* was spelt with a capital M and came to be regarded as nothing less than a god.

Our god is the power in whom we trust, and the one that we worship and serve. A man I know spent all his working life worrying about what would happen to him when he retired, and he put more and more money into pension funds. He wore a worried expression and old clothes because he didn't want to waste money on new ones.

Jesus is saying to us, 'Don't put your trust in money—put it in your heavenly Father. He feeds the birds and he will feed you'—which isn't to say that we are to sit around and do nothing. The blackbird who lives in my garden works quite hard most of the day towing worms out of the grass. But they are there for him to eat, and he doesn't stockpile them for the future.

Reflect

Do what Jesus suggested. Really look at the birds, and the beauty of their feathers— and at the beauty of the flowers...

That I may know him

Indeed I count everything as loss because of the surpassing worth of knowing Christ Jesus my Lord. For his sake I have suffered the loss of all things, and count them as refuse, in order that I may gain Christ and be found in him, not having a righteousness of my own, based on law, but that which is through faith in Christ, the righteousness from God that depends on faith; that I may know him and the power of his resurrection, and may share his sufferings, becoming like him in his death, that if possible I may attain the resurrection from the dead.

All the things that Paul had glorified in before were worthless to him—because of the all-surpassing worth of 'knowing Christ Jesus my Lord'. Paul is utterly consecrated to the Christ he adores and worships, and the deepest desire of his heart is to know him better—more and more deeply. But for that to happen—for Paul and for us—there has to be suffering. We undergo a process of stripping and purging—and it hurts.

Fairly soon after the start of my own Christian life I made those words of Paul into my own prayer: 'That I may know him and the power of his resurrection, and may share his sufferings, becoming like him in his death.' I prayed the first phrase with total commitment and enthusiasm. The next two phrases I was less enthusiastic about, since suffering didn't appeal to me very much and death didn't appeal to me at all. But I so wanted to know Christ, in the deepest way that it was ever possible for me (such as I am) to know him, that I was prepared to go along with the suffering and the death. And he takes us at our word even while he sympathizes with our feelings. He can lead us through the suffering of disappointed hopes and the death of human, and quite natural, desires, in order to give us the true and the deepest desire of our heart—which when it is prised out of the confusion of our divided hearts is always for the union and communion of love, with ourselves as beloved and also lover. It is only God with whom we can know that total love—always there, and there for always. It is only God who can deal with our inner loneliness and totally satisfy the desire of our heart for love.

A prayer

Pray those words of Paul for yourself...

The provision of God

Be careful to follow every command I am giving you today, so that you may live and increase and may enter and possess the land that the Lord promised on oath to your forefathers. Remember how the Lord your God led you all the way in the desert these forty years, to humble you and to test you in order to know what was in your heart, whether or not you would keep his commands. He humbled you, causing you to hunger and then feeding you with manna, which neither you nor your fathers had known, to teach you that man does not live on bread alone but on every word that comes from the mouth of the Lord.

There is a brand of Christianity that says that when a person becomes a Christian then God makes all their enterprises successful. He won't. It simply isn't true.

Those who know about the spiritual life tell us that we are 'stripped', and it is in this process of stripping and suffering that God finds out (and so do we) how much we really love him. Job said, 'Though he slay me yet will I trust in him' (Job 13:15). But it is harder when we are still alive and our life is going agonizingly wrong. The job that we love comes to an end. The person that we cherish doesn't love us. We become ill—or someone close to us does.

What then? Do we cry out, 'Why should this happen to me?' Or do we bow our heads to it and set about learning obedience through our suffering? There are, strictly, no second causes, because God created our world with all its possibilities for good and evil. But in all our suffering God is there with us. In *Making Sense out of Suffering* (Hodder) Peter Kreeft wrote that 'Suffering is not a problem requiring an answer but a mystery requiring a presence.'

To think about

What has caused most suffering in my life? Has this brought me closer to God—or have I somehow turned away from him into bitterness or unhappiness?

The sap of the Spirit

[Jesus said] 'I am the true vine, and my Father is the vinedresser. Every branch in me that bears no fruit he cuts away, and every branch that does bear fruit he prunes to make it bear even more. You are pruned already, by means of the word that I have spoken to you. Make your home in me, as I make mine in you. As a branch cannot bear fruit all by itself, but must remain part of the vine, neither can you unless you remain in me. I am the vine, you are the branches. Whoever remains in me, with me in him, bears fruit in plenty; for cut off from me you can do nothing.'

I was walking through a vineyard in Cyprus on a hot autumn day. There was a cloudless blue sky over my head, the earth was a beautiful, rich red, and as I walked I listened to the sound of the sea. The grapes had been harvested, but the low vines were still covered with lush green leaves on their short, twisted branches. All except one branch. That was covered in dry, brown leaves, and torn off from the vine. It was dead, and when the farmer came to get the vineyard ready for next year he would throw it away and burn it. No hope of that branch bearing a rich crop of grapes next year. The life-giving sap of the vine couldn't get through to it.

Before the next harvest, though, all the branches in all the vines would be fiercely pruned. Then they would bear fruit. A lot of fruit. Beautiful bunches of sweet, juicy grapes carried on the twisted branches of the vine. Branches that on the outside look dead and dry. But inside them the rich, life-giving sap of the vine is flowing through, from the roots to the fruit. Like the Holy Spirit of God...

So reflect on the sap and the Spirit—and on the fact that it is the Father who prunes the branches... you and me... through all the circumstances and the pain of our lives... through what the world and other people do to us... and through what we do (and fail to do) to other people. There is always pain in the pruning—but God is always there in the pain with us.

The
MERCY
of
GOD

The forgiveness of God

If we say that we have no sin, we deceive ourselves, and the truth is not in us. If we confess our sins, he who is faithful and just will forgive us our sins and cleanse us from all unrighteousness. If we say that we have not sinned, we make him a liar, and his word is not in us.

I once shared an open-plan office—and the person on the desk facing me was a militant atheist. Whenever I did anything that offended her she would shout out, 'That's not very Christian!' It felt a bit unfair. I was the only friend she had there—because she had quarrelled with everyone else. But she was (annoyingly) right. It wasn't very Christian to be short-tempered or irritable—and it definitely wasn't Christ-like.

But my irritability didn't mean that I wasn't a Christian. I was what 1 Peter 2:2 calls a newborn baby—newly converted to the faith, and with a lot of growing to do. A Christian sinner who kept getting it wrong—and whom God kept on forgiving. And however much we grow 'in grace and in the knowledge of him' we shall be sinners until the end of our Christian lives on this side of death—not one of us totally Christ-like or totally loving.

But we can't say, 'Well it doesn't matter if I sin, because I'll be forgiven anyway.' If we think like that then the reality of our Christian faith is doubtful. To be a Christian is to know God, to love God and other people (though not perfectly yet)—and to know and to mind that our lack of love grieves the Spirit. We are in a new relationship now with the God and Father of our Lord Jesus Christ. We are the sons and daughters of the living God: all of us forgiven sinners. Forgiven at the start of our Christian life, with the washing and the new birth symbolized in the sacrament of baptism. And forgiven every day of our Christian life—if we confess our sins, and if we forgive one another as God in Christ has forgiven us.

A prayer

Our Father in heaven... Forgive us our sins as we forgive those who sin against us. Amen.

John 14:15–20, 23 (NIV)

God with us

'If you love me, you will obey what I command. And I will ask the Father, and he will give you another Counsellor to be with you for ever—the Spirit of truth. The world cannot accept him, because it neither sees him nor knows him. But you know him, for he lives with you and will be in you. I will not leave you as orphans; I will come to you... Because I live, you also will live. On that day you will realize that I am in my Father, and you are in me, and I am in you... If anyone loves me, he will obey my teaching. My Father will love him, and we will come to him and make our home with him.

Christianity is about the amazing truth that the God who made the galaxies, and who holds the stars and all things in being by his word of power, comes to live within the human heart. Yes, Christianity is about the forgiveness of sins and the love of God as well—but the God who is creator and lover wants to live in union and communion with every one of his human creatures. The God of the galaxies is also the God within, if we will have him. Jesus says to his disciples (and to us), 'If you love me, you will obey what I command...' What he commands us to do is to believe in him, and in the glorious truth that he loves us and died for us, and that (if we ask) he will forgive us our sins—everything we have ever done in the past, and the sins that we go on sinning in the present even though we long not to give in. And with the first forgiveness, which is the start of our Christian life, a wiping out of the past, and a beautiful new beginning, Jesus asks the Father for a Counsellor to be with us for ever. The Father hears his request and pours out the Holy Spirit on the Day of Pentecost to create the church, and each of us needs our own, personal Pentecost. If we don't know the glory of it, Holy Communion can help us. As we eat the bread and drink the wine we can know in faith that God-in-Christ comes to us and stays with us for ever.

At long last

And God said to Abraham, 'As for Sarai, your wife, you shall not call her name Sarai, but Sarah shall be her name. I will bless her, and moreover I will give you a son by her; I will bless her, and she shall be a mother of nations...' Then Abraham fell on his face and laughed, and said to himself, 'Shall a child be born to a man who is a hundred years old? Shall Sarah, who is ninety years old, bear a child?' And Abraham said to God, 'O that Ishmael might live in thy sight!' God said, 'No, but Sarah your wife shall bear you a son, and you shall call his name Isaac... As for Ishmael, I have heard you; behold, I will bless him and... I will make him a great nation. But I will establish my covenant with Isaac, whom Sarah shall bear to you at this season next year.'

God gives Sarai a slightly changed name as a symbol of her share in the covenant he has made with Abraham. Both names mean 'princess'—and Sarah is going to be one. The blessing is to her as well as to Abraham, and she will be the mother of nations and of kings, through the baby son who is going to be born to her—to her, and not to anyone else. Ishmael will also be blessed (the promised blessing to Abraham flowing through both his sons)—but the greatest promise (and the promise impossible to fulfil except through the power of God) will flow through the son born when it is humanly speaking impossible. Abraham laughed at the sheer impossibility of it—but perhaps it was the laughter of delight. Of daring really to believe that the thing he had longed for through so many years was at last going to happen—the joy would well up inside him and become first of all a smile, and then the release of laughter. Now God had told him the time of the longed-for birth—and soon the long years of waiting and hoping would be over.

A prayer

Lord God, help me to believe your promises before they come true—and to act accordingly in the present.

You're great!

So if there is any encouragement in Christ, any incentive of love, any participation in the Spirit, any affection and sympathy, complete my joy by being of the same mind, having the same love, being in full accord and of one mind. Do nothing from selfishness or conceit, but in humility count others better than yourselves. Let each of you look not only to his own interests, but also to the interests of others.

Christians ought not to be selfish or conceited, but we often are. Our selfishness and conceit spoil and divide the Church, and the unbelievers look at us and laugh—not amused, but mocking and despising.

Love and unity are not automatic in the Christian life. We have to look to ourselves and to the Spirit to live out our new lives in Christ. We have to realize how much God loves us (which will mean reflecting on our faith, and knowing it, and praying it in) and then love other people with the same love.

When Paul says, 'In humility count others better than yourselves,' he isn't saying, 'Pretend...' that (for example) someone is a superb administrator when they are manifestly hopeless. If you or I are good at something then we can be pleased, and deeply thankful, and give God the glory for it. And we can be aware of our infinite importance and preciousness to God. Your soul is worth more than the whole world, and so is mine. We know that because Jesus said that if a man should gain the whole world and lose his own soul (or his true self) then he wouldn't make a profit but a loss.

But then we can forget about ourselves, for the time being, and put other people in the spotlight. We can delight in what they do—and even more in what they are: beloved children of God (and our brothers and sisters) and precious to him and to us. We can affirm them and tell them these things. It's a way of expressing love.

A reflection

Reflect on what it means to count others better than yourself, in humility. Think of your own value. Then think of a person you know, of whom you haven't a very high opinion. Pray for him, or for her, and spend some time thinking of that person's preciousness to God, and also what he or she is good at.

Surely not him, God?

Thus says the Lord to his anointed, to Cyrus, whose right hand I have grasped to subdue nations before him and strip kings of their robes, to open doors before him— and the gates shall not be closed: I will go before you... I will give you the treasures of darkness and riches hidden in secret places, so that you may know that it is I, the Lord, the God of Israel, who call you by your name. For the sake of my servant Jacob, and Israel my chosen, I call you by your name, I surname you, though you do not know me. I am the Lord, and there is no other; besides me there is no god.

God is far more generous-spirited than we are—and I have discovered over the years that he uses and works through people who, in my opinion, it would be better not to work through! I can think of one man who acted towards his wife in a most irritating and thoughtless way, but nevertheless God used him in an extraordinary way in ministering to people and speaking at meetings. I disapproved—both of the man's behaviour and of the way God saw fit to work through him! But I have become a bit wiser and a little more generous-spirited since the days of my deep disapproval, and I have realized that God will use anything and anybody that is available to him, even though their beliefs and their actions are far from perfect. Mary Poppins may be 'practically perfect always' when she measures herself against the rule of the good behaviour stick, but we live in the real world and we aren't. Yet God lavishes his love and his Spirit on us, and fills us with himself wherever there is a capacity for him. That is what he did with Cyrus, the pagan king of Babylon. God knew Cyrus, even though Cyrus didn't know him—at least not *then*, although perhaps he did later. We don't know, though he encouraged the rebuilding of the temple. Cyrus was 'the Lord's anointed'—which is just what the kings of Israel were. But perhaps it isn't so surprising. After all, God was Cyrus' creator— even if Cyrus didn't know that.

A reflection

Do you believe that God can only use people who have their Christian belief properly buttoned up and who are utterly orthodox? Do you believe that God can anoint a person of another faith with his Spirit—without interfering with their freedom? Do you find this a difficult passage? Bring your bewilderment (if you have any) to God—and praise him anyway—for the wonder of his love, for the mercy of his acceptance and forgiveness, and for the glory of his creation.

How can we know?

[Jesus said] 'You know the way to the place where I am going.' Thomas said to him, 'Lord, we don't know where you are going, so how can we know the way?' Jesus answered, 'I am the way and the truth and the life. No one comes to the Father except through me.'

I love the way that Thomas is brave enough to contradict Jesus. 'You know the way to the place where I am going,' says Jesus, and Thomas immediately says, 'How can we? We don't know *where* you are going!' It's a valid point. But if Thomas had really been listening to what Jesus had just been saying, then he would have known. Jesus is going to his Father's house. There are many rooms there (and one of them would be Thomas' room—a place for Thomas). The way into the Father's house is through the Son—and earlier on in John's Gospel Jesus has used the picture of a sheepfold and a shepherd: 'I tell you the truth, I am the gate for the sheep... whoever enters through me will be saved. He will come in and go out, and find pasture... I have come that they may have life, and have it to the full. I am the good shepherd. The good shepherd lays down his life for the sheep' (John 10:7, 9–11).

The Son who is the good shepherd will give his life for the sheep. But he isn't a dead shepherd or a dead son. He's alive! (They don't know that yet, but they will.) God the Son is the true (not false) and living (not dead) way to God the Father. Perhaps we don't have to 'be a Christian' to come to God. But whoever comes must know something of the true nature of God—that she or he comes to a God who is loving, merciful and forgiving. No one can thrust into the holy presence of God holding out the entry ticket of their own good life. Merit won't get anyone in. But I believe that the mercy of God will let anyone in who asks for that mercy.

A prayer

Lord Jesus, help me to listen to you—and to ask you questions (like Thomas) when I don't understand (and when perhaps I haven't listened). Thank you that you are the way, the truth and the life—and that you are merciful. Amen.

The Shepherd

*The Lord is my shepherd, I shall not want. He maketh me to lie down in green
pastures: he leadeth me beside the still waters. He restoreth my soul...*

This is the best-loved of all the Psalms. We sing it at our weddings and at
our funerals and the words bring us comfort and joy. We always think of it
as the Shepherd Psalm, but the Shepherd is also the Guide and the Host.
It has just one theme, that God is sufficient for all our human need.

Flocks in the Middle East follow the shepherd, who leads them into the
pastures where they will find just the food they needed. And whatever is
happening to us right now is just the food that we need—even though we
might not like the taste of it very much.

The shepherd is in the process of restoring 'my soul', which often
means 'my life' or 'myself'. God restores and renews *me*. A few years ago
I watched them restoring Michelangelo's marvellous ceiling in the Sistine
Chapel. They were half way through and the colours at one end were dark
and the colours at the other bright. The dirt and grime of the years had
dulled the original painting, but now all the figures were being restored
to their original glory.

In God's original design he created us in his own image and likeness.
But as one of the confessions puts it, 'we have marred your image within
us'. God can then restore it to the original design. The Shepherd God has
glorious plans for his sheep!

To think about

Wherever he may guide me,
No want shall turn me back;
My Shepherd is beside me
And nothing can I lack.
His wisdom ever waketh,
His sight is never dim;
He knows the way he taketh,
And I will walk with him.

A.L. Waring

Accept the place the divine providence has found for you, the society of your
contemporaries, the connection of events.

Ralph Waldo Emerson

He was made sin for us

Yet it was the will of the Lord to bruise him; he has put him to grief; when he makes himself an offering for sin, he shall see his offspring, he shall prolong his days; the will of the Lord shall prosper in his hand; he shall see the fruit of the travail of his soul and be satisfied; by his knowledge shall the righteous one, my servant, make many to be accounted righteous; and he shall bear their iniquities.

This astonishing suffering of the servant of the Lord is the will of the Lord. This is the way the sorrows of the world are going to be transmuted into joy. This is the way the sins of the word are going to be forgiven. And after he has made himself 'an offering for sin' he will see his sons and daughters. A strange progression, because the sin offering was always put to death. The bull offered on the Day of Atonement was killed, and the High Priest sprinkled its blood over the people. The Passover lamb was killed and eaten, and its blood put on the door-posts so that the angel of death would 'pass over' the house.

In Leviticus 5:14–19 a man who is guilty of sin 'shall bring to the priest a ram without blemish... and the priest shall make atonement for him... it is a guilt offering.' The guilt offering is a substitute for the guilty person. The one who is guilty is the one who ought to die—but God accepts a substitute. And when John the Baptist saw Jesus coming towards him at the start of his ministry he said, 'Behold, the Lamb of God, who takes away the sin of the world!' (John 1:29)

Just a few days ago someone told me how he resented God, because God was so cruel and condemning. I found myself with tears in my eyes, saying, 'I can hardly bear what you say—and I am not blaming you, but you have got it hopelessly and utterly wrong.' God makes the innocent and obedient servant into the 'sin offering', and the ram without blemish pours out his life, and his blood, even unto death. But the picture of an unloving and angry Father pouring out his wrath on a loving and innocent Son is distorted.

A reflection

...in Christ God was (or, God was in Christ) reconciling the world to himself (2 Corinthians 5:19).

Now I know I am . . .

For you did not receive the spirit of slavery to fall back into fear, but you have received
the spirit of sonship. When we cry, 'Abba! Father!' it is the Spirit himself bearing
witness with our spriit that we are children of God, and if children, then heirs, heirs
of God and fellow heirs with Christ, provided we suffer with him in order that we
may also be glorified with him.

The Spirit in the heart of the Christian is the Spirit of the Son of God—and
Jesus called his Father 'Abba'. It is the word that a little child uses—like our
English word 'Daddy'. When we find ourselves crying out to God like that,
we know that we have an inner witness to the truth that we are children
of God.

Some years ago my father and I heard Dr Martyn Lloyd-Jones preaching on the doctrine of assurance. As he drove the car towards Hyde Park
Corner my father was smiling. 'I know now that I'm a Christian,' he told
me. 'You told me I was, and I didn't believe you. But now I know.' Next
morning I took him in a cup of tea and he was sitting up in bed waiting
for it and looking happy. 'When I woke up this morning I knew that something nice had happened. But for a moment I couldn't remember what.
Then I did remember. I know now that I am a Christian.' Two years after
that, just two months after his seventieth birthday, he died. He was quite
sure that he was a Christian—a forgiven sinner and a child of God. His two
favourite books in the Bible were the letter to the Romans and the book
of Revelation. He read them alternately over his morning tea and loved
them—and as he read his faith grew deeper and stronger.

A story my father loved

The famous preacher D.L. Moody once said this to his congregation. 'One morning
you will read in the paper, "Moody is dead." But don't you believe it! On that
morning I shall be more alive than I have ever been.'

My body and my blood

I have just come back from Holy Communion and am deeply aware, for the thousandth time, of the wonder and superb symbolism of the sacrament that Jesus gave to us. I held out my hands to receive the bread and put it in my mouth. I chewed it, then I swallowed it. After that I drank the red wine from the silver cup. And both the body and blood of Christ became part of my body and blood.

Ever since I set out to follow Christ and invited him to enter my heart, I have believed that he is with me. But this reminder and remembrance is a powerful sacrament of the glory of the Christian life. Paul wrote to the Colossians about the riches of the glory of the mystery which God had made known, 'which is Christ in you, the hope of glory' (1:27). To touch the bread, and to be aware of it becoming part of me as I eat it, and to feel the wine in my mouth, entering me and becoming my being, is a unique strengthening and empowering. The Christ who gave us that sacrament '...opened wide his arms for us on the cross; he put an end to death by dying for us and revealed the resurrection by rising to new life...' (*ASB* Third Eucharistic Prayer).

The Christ who is with us, and in us, shares our suffering—and the bread and the wine in our bodies remind us that we are the body of Christ. Paul says that he received his teaching about Holy Communion direct from the risen Christ.

For I received from the Lord what I also delivered to you, that the Lord Jesus on the night when he was betrayed took bread, and when he had given thanks, he broke it, and said, 'This is my body which is for you. Do this in remembrance of me.' In the same way also the cup, after supper, saying, 'This cup is the new covenant in my blood. Do this, as often as you drink it, in remembrance of me.' For as often as you eat this bread and drink the cup, you proclaim the Lord's death until he comes.

Really alive

Are there any situations in your life that seem absolutely hopeless? A broken relationship, perhaps… that once was alive and exciting, but now it's dead. Your church perhaps… that never seems to have been alive, or if it was you weren't there to enjoy it. As you look at the situation you haven't much hope… only a deep sadness. That's how Ezekiel must have felt. But then God spoke to him in a vision—and in some churches it is read out on Easter Eve, the night before the resurrection.

The hand of the Lord was upon me, and he brought me out by the Spirit of the Lord, and set me down in the midst of the valley; it was full of bones … and lo, they were very dry. And he said to me, 'Son of man, can these bones live?' And I answered, 'O Lord God, thou knowest.' Again he said to me, 'Prophesy to these bones, and say to them, O dry bones, hear the word of the Lord … I will cause breath to enter you, and you shall live…' So I prophesied as I was commanded; and as I prophesied, there was a noise, and behold, a rattling; and the bones came together, bone to its bone. And as I looked, there were sinews on them, and flesh had come upon them, and skin had covered them; but there was no breath in them. Then he said to me, 'Prophesy to the breath; prophesy, son of man, and say to the breath, Thus says the Lord God: Come from the four winds, O breath, and breathe upon these slain, that they may live.' So I prophesied as he commanded me, and the breath came into them, and they lived, and stood upon their feet, an exceedingly great host.

A way to pray

Shut your eyes and see the valley of dry bones… coming to life… see the breath of God breathing new life into the ones who had been dead… making them fully alive… Then hold your dead and hopeless situation… or someone else's… in the presence of God… and pray that he will put together the broken pieces and then breathe the breath of life into them.

O Breath of Life, come sweeping through us,
revive thy church with life and power,
O Breath of Life, come cleanse, renew us,
and fit thy church to meet this hour.

Elizabeth Porter Head

To purify me

Then Job replied: 'Even today my complaint is bitter; his hand is heavy in spite of my groaning. If only I knew where to find him; if only I could go to his dwelling... But if I go to the east, he is not there; if I go to the west, I do not find him. When he is at work in the north, I do not see him; when he turns to the south, I catch no glimpse of him. But he knows the way that I take; when he has tested me, I shall come forth as gold.

If we can hold on to Job's understanding when we are in our own furnace of affliction we shall never totally lose hope. God did not seem to be present for Job. Nor for C.S. Lewis, after his wife died: 'Go to Him when your need is desperate, when all other help is vain, and what do you find? A door slammed in your face, and a sound of bolting and double-bolting on the inside. After that, silence...' (*A Grief Observed*) Even for Jesus, crying out on the cross, 'My God, my God, why have you forsaken me?'

But neither Job nor C.S. Lewis nor Jesus stopped believing in God. What they were experiencing—in different degrees—was the agony of his absence when they had known the joy of his presence. But what gives hope in the agony is the belief that somehow, through it all, the purposes of God are being accomplished. Jesus' triumphant cry at the end: 'It is finished!' The work of sin-bearing was completed. He said he had come 'not to be served but to serve, and to give his life as a ransom for many'. Now he had done it. Now we can know forgiveness and 'the fellowship of his suffering'—the knowledge that God-in-Christ has entered into the depth of our suffering and dereliction. 'God was in Christ, reconciling the world to himself...' (2 Corinthians 5:19). That was the purpose of Christ's suffering on the cross. The purpose of ours is to purify us—and even in his pain Job held on to that: 'When he has tested me, I shall come forth as gold'. God knew what he was doing with Job.

Reflect

Green pastures are before me,
Which yet I have not seen;
Bright skies will soon be o'er me,
Where the dark clouds have been.
My hope I cannot measure;
My path to life is free;
My Saviour has my treasure,
And he will walk with me.

A.L. Waring

Because I sinned

Some terrible things happen to us because of what other people have done. Others happen because of what we have done. They are God's judgment on our sin, and once we have managed to admit the sin we can see the logic of the judgment. After King David's appalling sin God sent the prophet Nathan to him to tell him a story about a rich man and a poor man who had a little ewe lamb...

'...*He raised it, and it grew up with him and his children. It shared his food, drank from his cup and even slept in his arms. It was like a daughter to him. Now a traveller came to the rich man, but the rich man refrained from taking one of his own sheep or cattle to prepare a meal for the traveller... Instead, he took the ewe lamb that belonged to the poor man...' David burned with anger against the man... 'As surely as the Lord lives, the man who did this deserves to die!'... Then Nathan said to David, 'You are the man! ... You struck down Uriah the Hittite with the sword and took his wife to be your own... Now, therefore, the sword shall never depart from your house, because you despised (the Lord) and took the wife of Uriah the Hittite to be your own.'*

David despised God and destroyed Uriah. He repented. But once you have killed someone you cannot bring them back to life, however sorry you are. God forgave David, and their relationship was restored—as David cried out for it to be in his great penitential psalm: 'Do not cast me from your presence, or take your Holy Spirit from me. Restore to me the joy of your salvation...' (51:11–12). But life would never be the same again. For David's own good he would have to suffer the consequences of his actions, even though he would know the presence of God with him in his sufferings. David had used violence to gain his own ends. Now there would be violence in his own household.

To think about

Over and over again, as we break some rule which seems rather arbitrary and meaningless, we discover the principle which had dictated it. We set in motion the causes and effects from which we understand, for the first time, why there had ever been that prohibition;then it is too late. The discovery is called the Fall of Man.

William Temple, *Christian Faith and Life*

A meal with God

(Jesus) went away to the lake-side. All the crowd came to him, and he taught them there. As he went along, he saw Levi son of Alphaeus at his seat in the custom-house, and said to him, 'Follow me'; and Levi rose and followed him. When Jesus was at table in his house, many bad characters—tax-gatherers and others—were seated with him and his disciples; for there were many who followed him. Some doctors of the law who were Pharisees noticed him eating in this bad company, and said to his disciples, 'He eats with tax-gatherers and sinners!' Jesus heard it and said to them, 'It is not the healthy that need a doctor, but the sick; I did not come to invite virtuous people, but sinners.'

Recently a Christian woman, who wasn't married, told me in great distress that she had had an abortion. She was crippled with guilt, and had left her home and her church and moved to a place where no one knew her. 'I have tried to pray,' she told me, 'and to ask for forgiveness, but it feels as if God isn't listening to me.' She knows that what she has done is irreversible. She can't bring her tiny, unborn child back to life again and she can't bring herself to go to church again.

I listened to her pain and then gently reminded her of the passage that is the Gospel for today. Jesus eats with sinners (some of them were prostitutes), and he invites sinners to eat with him. I suggested that she went to Holy Communion—and that as she went up she should remind herself that she was going to eat at table with Jesus, and that he was coming to eat with her—just as he did with all sorts of sinners when he was here on earth.

I also suggested that she should tell Jesus all about her distress and her pain and her guilt—and then imagine how he must have looked at the woman they brought to him who had been caught in the act of adultery. I believe that there would have been compassion and tenderness and an enormous kindness in his face. Then, perhaps, she could curl up by her bed and (as it were) weep on his shoulder, and weep for her child.

Ask for God

(Jesus) was praying in a certain place, and after he had finished, one of his disciples said to him, 'Lord, teach us to pray, as John taught his disciples.' He said to them, 'When you pray, say: Father, hallowed be your name. Your kingdom come. Give us each day our daily bread. And forgive us our sins, for we ourselves forgive everyone indebted to us. And do not bring us to the time of trial ... So I say to you, Ask, and it will be given you; search, and you will find; knock, and the door will be opened for you. For everyone who asks receives; and everyone who searches finds; and for everyone who knocks, the door will be opened. Is there anyone among you who, if your child asks for a fish, will give a snake instead of a fish? Or if the child asks for an egg, will give a scorpion? If you then, who are evil, know how to give good gifts to your children, how much more will the heavenly Father give the Holy Spirit to those who ask him!'

'When you go to the library,' my next door neighbour said to me, 'please will you bring me back the further education leaflet.' She has already been to a beginners' class in calligraphy, and now she wants to move on to the next stage. It is like that with prayer. We start as beginners—and we learn how to pray like a child learning to speak. Part of the prayer is simply the pleasure of being in the presence of God—just as a baby loves to be held by its mother or father. The start of a new relationship—and then the language to be learned in order to communicate. Listening—and speaking. A crying out that we are hungry and thirsty—and a quiet resting when we are satisfied. '...I have stilled and quietened my soul; like a weaned child with its mother, like a weaned child is my soul within me' (Psalm 131:2, NIV).

But we have to move on. The disciples must have known something about praying. But they wanted to know more and so they asked for help. Right at the heart of praying there is our Father God—far better than any human father. But we can learn something of what God is like by looking at how human fathers (and mothers) act towards their children. No human parent would give a child a snake instead of a fish. But what if the child asked for a snake, something that would damage it and harm it? Then the answer will be 'No', and the thing we long for won't be given to us. But something and someone far better will be given. We can ask for the Spirit—who is the living God himself. And day after day he will keep on coming to us, and keep on filling us with himself and the glory of his living presence. So ask—and know that to this request the answer is always 'Yes'.

Entitled to say so

I therefore, the prisoner in the Lord, beg you to lead a life worthy of the calling to which you have been called, with all humility and gentleness, with patience, bearing with one another in love, making every effort to maintain the unity of the Spirit in the bond of peace. There is one body and one Spirit, just as you were called to the one hope of your calling, one Lord, one faith, one baptism, one God and Father of all, who is above all and through all and in all.

A brilliant professor whom I know spends most of his days and nights looking after his wife, who has Alzheimer's disease. He is 85 and she is 83—and his patience and gentleness are astonishing. When I go to stay with them I watch him caring for her, and doing all that has to be done for her and for the housekeeping as well. And I remember the impatience of his earlier years and I am wide-eyed at the grace of God working in him. So if he should ever try to prod me towards patience (an area where I need a lot of help!) I would listen—because he knows the way to it and he knows what he is talking about. It is just like that with Paul. Writing from the cell of a Roman prison, he was entitled to beg people to live a life worthy of the calling they had been called to. He was in far worse circumstances than theirs.

In the daily nit-picking and criticism that goes on in the average church Paul's words might shame us into repentance. 'I don't get anything out of it,' some people complain after a service. To which the reply has to be: 'And what did you put into it?' Catherine Marshall was once deeply convicted of her critical tongue and her critical attitude to other people—and she prayed for forgiveness and a new attitude. Perhaps if we do the same, God could use us more effectively—and the world would see the Christ-likeness of Christians in the Church of Christ.

A way to pray

Ask yourself, 'Is my life worthy of the calling to which I have been called? Am I like Christ? Do I make every (or any) effort to maintain the unity of the Spirit in the bond of peace? Do I need to repent?'

Rejoice!

*Rejoice in the Lord always; again I will say, Rejoice. Let all men know your forbear-
ance. The Lord is at hand. Have no anxiety about anything, but in eveything by
prayer and supplication with thanksgiving let your requests be made known to God.*

Today we look at Paul's teaching about our relationships and our circumstances. Because of our relationship with God we are to rejoice. If we
reflect on the wonder of it, day by day, then our hearts will be full to over-
flowing with praise and delight: 'Ransomed, healed, restored, forgiven,
Who like me his praise should sing?' (J. Newton) Because of that, our relationship with all people has to be characterized by a gracious gentleness.
Forbearance can make us think of someone pursing their lips rather dis-
approvingly, to show that they are somehow managing to be patient with
a person who is causing them considerable irritation. But the real meaning of the word is someone who knows how to temper justice with mercy.
A person like Jesus—who didn't apply the letter of the law to the woman
taken in adultery. He didn't condone it. He said, 'Go, and sin no more.'
(John 8:11, AV) And perhaps, because he was merciful, she didn't—or not
in that way. Perhaps she followed Jesus and had all her sins forgiven. It
doesn't say and we don't know. But we do know how Christ showed forbearance—not with the pursed lips of disapproval, but with love and
mercy.

Our relationship with God will make a radical difference to our circumstances. First of all we rejoice in the God who loves us and forgives
us—and we think about what our God is like. That's easy—because he is
like Jesus. 'He who has seen me has seen the Father...' (John 14:9). And
Jesus taught us how to pray, and to say 'Our Father...' So we aren't to be
anxious, and we're to pray about everything. Everything that matters to us
matters to our heavenly Father. Nothing is too big and nothing is too
small. So...

A way to pray

*Pray about everything that makes you anxious—and everything that's in your heart.
'And the peace of God, which passes all understanding, will keep your hearts and your
minds in Christ Jesus.' (Philippians 4:7)*

He carried it for us

All we like sheep have gone astray; we have turned every one to his own way; and the Lord has laid on him the iniquity of us all. He was oppressed, and he was afflicted, yet he opened not his mouth; like a lamb that is led to the slaughter, and like a sheep that before its shearers is dumb, so he opened not his mouth.

In my Bible alongside today's reading there is a drawing of a sheep standing on a tiny ledge at the edge of a precipice. It is in great danger, and there is no way for it to rescue itself. Unless the shepherd lays on an astonishing rescue operation the sheep is facing certain death. Isaiah is saying that God has done just what a good shepherd always does. He has laid on a rescue operation for all his lost sheep (and all of us are lost, or are until he has found us) that will mean life instead of death for us. But the cost is enormous. 'I am the good shepherd,' Jesus said. 'The good shepherd lays down his life for the sheep' (John 10:11).

Today's verses are very special to me, because it was through them that I discovered how my sins could be forgiven (and through Revelation 3:20 that I invited into my heart the one who forgave me and died in order to do it). 'Do you realize that you are a sinner?' the Reverend John Collins asked me, looking at me with an immensely kind expression. 'Of course I do,' I told him. 'Hold out your hands,' John said, and on one of them he placed a heavy Bible. 'This hand is you,' he told me, 'and the Bible is your sin. Your other, empty, hand is Jesus. Now listen…' He read aloud to me, 'All we like sheep have gone astray; we have turned every one to his own way; and the Lord has laid on him the iniquity of us all'—and as he said those last words he removed the heavy 'sin' from the hand that was me and put it on the hand that was Jesus. 'Now where is your sin?' he asked me. A child could have told him. 'It's on Jesus.'

A thought

Led like a lamb to the slaughter
In silence and shame,
There on Your back You carried a world
Of violence and pain.
Bleeding, dying, bleeding, dying…

Graham Kendrick

Extract from 'Led like a lamb to the slaughter' by Graham Kendrick, copyright © 1983 Kingsway's Thankyou Music, PO Box 75, Eastbourne, East Sussex, BN23 6NW, UK. Used by permission.

Show me!

*What good is it, my brothers and sisters, if you say you have faith but do not have
works? Can faith save you? If a brother or sister is naked and lacks daily food,
and one of you says to them, 'Go in peace; keep warm and eat your fill,' and yet you
do not supply their bodily needs, what is the good of that? So faith by itself, if it has
no works, is dead. But someone will say, 'You have faith and I have works.' Show me
your faith apart from your works, and I by my works will show you my faith. You
believe that God is one; you do well. Even the demons believe—and shudder.*

I am sitting in my garden as I write these notes, under a clear blue sky, and
the late summer sunshine is ripening the heavy crop of blackberries on the
bush which covers half my garden fence. Every year it gives a rich harvest
to me and my friends—to make into bramble jelly, blackberry fool and
blackberry and apple pie (which I like made with short pastry and served
with double cream). The apples grow on a tree in the same border. But in
a bucket by my back door there is a small blackberry bush with a big, dead
branch on it—which will never bear a sweet, ripe blackberry.

A living faith isn't just about words, but about actions. Like Eliza
Doolittle in a rage with Freddie in the musical *My Fair Lady*:

'Words, words, words, I'm so sick of words. I get words all day through,
first from him, now from you. Is that all you blighters can do? Don't talk
of stars, burning above. If you're in love—Show me!'

Words aren't enough. Belief in God isn't enough either. 'The demons
believe—and tremble,' says James. If I just believe that my blackberries
and apples are good for food it won't do me or my friends any good—only
if I pick them and we eat them in a delicious pie.

A thought

*'O taste and see that the Lord is good' (Psalm 34:8). Think about how you do
that—and how you turn your living faith into loving works and actions.*

With confidence

Therefore, since we have a great high priest who has gone through the heavens, Jesus the Son of God, let us hold firmly to the faith we profess. For we do not have a high priest who is unable to sympathize with our weaknesses, but we have one who has been tempted in every way, just as we are—yet was without sin. Let us then approach the throne of grace with confidence, so that we may receive mercy and find grace to help us in our time of need.

There are some doors that I can knock on with absolute confidence. I know that the friend inside will be glad to see me—and will hold the door wide open and ask me to come in. Then I shall be offered something to drink and probably something to eat as well. Nearly all of us can go with confidence into a few places. But the marvel is that we can go to the throne of the universe with total confidence at any time.

The writer to the Hebrews is using the picture of the Jewish temple. The high priest could only go into the holiest place of all, where the presence of God dwelt, once a year, bearing the blood of sacrifice. But now Jesus is the great high priest who has gone into the presence of God on our behalf through the blood of his own sacrifice. The way into the presence of God is not closed any more. It is open—for ever. So we can come to God with confidence. Like Wesley's marvellous hymn: 'Bold, I approach the eternal throne, And claim the crown, through Christ my own.' Added to that, our high priest and our mediator utterly understands our human weaknesses and temptations, because he has been through all of them—but without giving in to them. He understands us and loves us—and in any temptation or distress we can approach the throne of grace and get all the help we need. If we want it… and if we ask…

Pray

Go now with confidence to the throne of grace, through Christ our great high priest, and ask for any help that you need…

In anguish and complaint

'Therefore I will not restrain my mouth; I will speak in the anguish of my spirit; I will complain in the bitterness of my soul. Am I the Sea, or the Dragon, that you set a guard over me? When I say, 'My bed will comfort me, my couch will ease my complaint,' then you scare me with dreams and terrify me with visions, so that I would choose strangling and death rather than this body. I loathe my life; I would not live forever. Let me alone, for my days are a breath.'

We can tell God everything that we are feeling. He knows all that we feel and all that we think anyway, and utterly understands us. But we still need to speak out. Not for his benefit but for ours. It is the truth that sets people free—so expressing the truth about our thoughts and feelings is a vital step on the way to our freedom and healing. Even God cannot do anything with our anger or our bitterness if we pretend that we are not angry, and not bitter. It is like confessing our sins. It is only when we recognize them and name them that we know the enormous relief of having them forgiven.

Until I was thirty years old I was never angry. Or at least, I never knew I was and never expressed it. Instead I had a series of agonizing bilious attacks, which knotted me and my stomach up in acute pain. Then, one day, I did get angry... really angry... and it was the day of my liberation, when my bilious attacks disappeared for ever. Now I express my anger (and all my other emotions) to God, just as Job did. At the end of the book God tells his friends that they got it wrong: 'You have not spoken of me what is right, *as my servant Job has*' (42:7). Job has spoken out plainly and openly to God. But the other side of the coin—the shining side—is that God has spoken plainly and openly to Job.

A way to pray

Try to get in touch with your feelings. Your disappointments... your anger... your sadness. Then 'feel' them in the presence of God—and tell him all about them. But then be quiet and listen. And go on doing this, day after day, for the rest of your life...

Not lost any more

Now the tax collectors and sinners were all drawing near to hear him. And the Pharisees and the scribes murmured, saying, 'This man receives sinners and eats with them.'

This marvellous chapter in Luke about lost things and lost people starts with a criticism of Jesus. But what the Pharisees said about him is very good news to those of us who know that we are sinners. And we all are. As a Christian friend of mine who is an alcoholic said to me, 'I shall never be able to say, "I was an alcoholic." I *am* one, and I always shall be. And it is like that with being a sinner, isn't it?' There is all the difference in the world between a sinner who doesn't know that she is, and one who does know and has been and is being forgiven.

The tax collectors and prostitutes whom Jesus received, and with whom he ate, were forgiven sinners. Once they were lost, but now they were found—by the Saviour of the world who had come to do just that. 'The Son of man is come to seek and to save that which was lost...'

A lost thing isn't fulfilling its purpose. When I lose my stamps (which usually live under a tray on my hall table, but sometimes stray into other places where I can't find them) they cannot be stuck on my letters to show the Post Office that I have paid the price of the postage. When a person is lost he or she isn't fulfilling his or her purpose either—and that purpose is to be a son or a daughter of God, and to live in a loving relationship with God for ever and ever. The Westminster Confession says that 'the chief end of man is to know God and to enjoy him for ever'. Now the tax collectors and the sinners were starting to know God, and God in Christ was receiving them and eating with them.

'Draw near with faith' it says in the Communion Service Book of Common Prayer, 'and take this holy sacrament to your comfort...' A ritualized form of the wonder of what happened, and what still happens, when sinners draw near to God in Christ.

A prayer

Saviour of the world, I am so glad that you have found me. I am so glad that you receive sinners and eat with them... that you receive me, and eat with me...

Where the blessing begins

Now the Lord said to Abram, 'Go from your country and your kindred and your father's house to the land that I will show you. And I will make of you a great nation, and I will bless you, and make your name great, so that you will be a blessing. I will bless those who bless you, and him who curses you I will curse; and by you all the families of the earth shall bless themselves.'

The Bible is full of new beginnings and fresh starts. They happen at just the critical time—at the point of a person's or a nation's greatest need. At every new beginning a human being hears the voice of God and obeys it. If they disobey, there is no new start and no blessing. Abram hears and obeys, and the blessing of God starts to flow like a river—not just to him but to the whole of the world.

The word bless (or blessing) comes five times in this passage, and God is the one who blesses. When a person is blessed it means that those things happen to them which are conducive to their happiness. When Jesus began the Sermon on the Mount with the beatitudes, he was telling us how we can be really blessed and really happy. The promise that God made to Abram had three parts to it. He would make him a great nation, he would give him a great name, and he would give him such a relationship with himself that through it all the families of the earth would bless themselves. The relationship is crucial to the blessing—for Abraham and for us.

A prayer

Lord God, thank you for Abraham's relationship with you—and the blessing it brought to the world. Help me always to hear your voice—always to follow you—wherever you call me to go. Thank you for all the new beginnings and new starts that happen in my life. Not just in the big things, but in the small, ordinary, day to day things like painting the living-room or just waking up in the morning to a new day. Be there for me Lord, in my beginnings and in my endings. Bless me—and bless others through me.

Forgiveness and fruit

For this reason, since the day we heard about you, we have not stopped praying for you and asking God to fill you with the knowledge of his will through all spiritual wisdom and understanding. And we pray this in order that you may live a life worthy of the Lord and may please him in every way: bearing fruit in every good work, growing in the knowledge of God, being strengthened with all power according to his glorious might so that you may have great endurance and patience, and joyfully giving thanks to the Father, who has qualified you to share in the inheritance of the saints in the kingdom of light. For he has rescued us from the dominion of darkness and brought us into the kingdom of the Son he loves, in whom we have redemption, the forgiveness of sins.

Our prayers start well and then fizzle out. But Paul's went on and on. And he kept on praying the same things. He asked God to fill the Colossians with a knowledge of his will—so that there were no gaps in their understanding and no places in their hearts and minds that didn't know what the will of God was. He asked that their lives would shine with the glory of God and be fruitful, as Jesus had told them to be: 'I am the vine; you are the branches. If a man remains in me and I in him, he will bear much fruit; apart from me you can do nothing... This is to my Father's glory, that you bear much fruit, showing yourselves to be my disciples' (John 15:5, 8).

Paul's prayer ends with great joy and thankfulness because of what has happened to him and to those he's praying for—and it has happened to all Christians too. We have all been rescued from the power of darkness and brought into the kingdom of light. The light of the world shines on us and in our hearts and gives us the power to love. We have all had our sins forgiven—so it isn't presumptuous to say that we know we are Christians. A Christian is a forgiven sinner whom God loves. Will you pray Paul's prayer again now for someone you know—and for yourself as well?

The river of life

On the last day of the feast, the great day, Jesus stood up and proclaimed, 'If any one thirst, let him come to me and drink. He who believes in me, as the scripture has said, "Out of his heart shall flow rivers of living water."' Now this he said about the Spirit, which those who believed in him were to receive; for as yet the Spirit had not been given, because Jesus was not yet glorified.

In Ezekiel's vision the river of life flows from the throne of God. It gets deeper all the way, and the man who speaks to Ezekiel in the vision tells him that when the river 'enters the stagnant waters of the sea, the water will become fresh. And wherever the river goes every living creature which swarms will live, and there will be very many fish; for this water goes there, that the waters of the sea may become fresh; so everything will live where the river goes' (Ezekiel 47:8–9).

Imagine having a river like that in our polluted world with its poisoned seas. A river of life that flows into the damaged places and makes them whole; that flows into the dead places and makes them alive. A river that flows into dirty, degraded souls and washes them clean and makes them alive with the life of God.

That is what Jesus offers us—if we want it. If we thirst for it. First of all the washing and the healing of our own souls. Then the flowing out of the river of life through us into the world that he loves and that he died for.

It starts with those who believe in Jesus: 'Those who have come to Him, and have had their own thirst quenched, that is to know what it means to have received the gift of the living water, that has become in them a well of water, springing up, laughing up, bubbling up, for ever springing, beautifying, satisfying...' (Campbell Morgan). And then the river of life flows out of us—living water for a dead world.

A prayer

Lord Jesus Christ, I believe in you. I come to you and I drink—and I believe your promise that out of me, and out of all who believe in you, rivers of living water will flow into your polluted, damaged, beloved world.

Mending the broken world

For it was not to angels that God subjected the world to come, of which we are speaking. It has been testified somewhere,

> *'What is man that thou art mindful of him,*
> *or the son of man, that thou carest for him?*
> *Thou didst make him for a little while lower than the angels;*
> *thou hast crowned him with glory and honour*
> *putting everything in subjection under his feet.'*

Now in putting everything in subjection to him, he left nothing outside his control. As it is, we do not yet see everything in subjection to him. But we see Jesus, who for a little while was made lower than the angels, crowned with glory and honour because of the suffering of death, so that by the grace of God he might taste death for every one.

Psalm 8 (which this passage quotes) is all about the glory that God has given to man. God put the whole world at his feet for him to have dominion over—and for woman to have dominion over as well, because 'God created man in his own image... male and female he created them' (Genesis 1:27). It was meant to be a loving dominion that blessed the whole earth with the love of God. But man (and woman) got it wrong. Their story, and the whole of history, is the story of broken relationships and a broken world.

So Jesus came to put it right: to remake the broken world and to bind up the broken-hearted. Jesus was made man—just like us. Now he is crowned with glory and honour, because he suffered death for us. William Barclay writes that 'Jesus Christ died to make man what he ought to be. Jesus Christ died to rid man of his frustration and his servitude and his bondage and his weakness and to give him the dominion he ought to have. Jesus Christ died to recreate man until man became the creature he was originally created to be. (*Daily Study Bible*)

Prayer

Jesus, Son of Man and Son of God, make me what you created me to be.

I want to see

They came to Jericho, and as Jesus was leaving with his disciples and a large crowd, a blind beggar named Bartimaeus... was sitting by the road. When he heard that it was Jesus of Nazareth, he began to shout, 'Jesus! Son of David! Take pity on me!' Many of the people scolded him and told him to be quiet. But he shouted even more loudly, 'Son of David, take pity on me!' Jesus stopped and said, 'Call him.' So they called to the blind man. 'Cheer up!' they said. 'Get up, he is calling you.' He threw off his cloak, jumped up, and came to Jesus. 'What do you want me to do for you?' Jesus asked him. 'Teacher,' the blind man answered, 'I want to see again.' 'Go,' Jesus told him, 'your faith has made you well.' At once he was able to see and followed Jesus on the road.

In my church there is a man of 85 years old who was a distinguished surgeon at a famous London hospital. A lifetime of healing—superb diagnosis, accurate incisions, delicate stitching—and to do that he had to see clearly. Now he can hardly see at all. Not even to read his beloved Bible, that he has studied and delighted in for the whole of his life. He has prayed just as Bartimaeus prayed: 'Lord, I want to see.' But he can't. Neither can thousands of other blind people—men and women and children all over the world. Victims of bilharzia and other water-related diseases (80 per cent of all blindness in Africa comes from water-related diseases). The many Christians among the blind must have prayed Bartimaeus' prayer: 'Lord, I want to see...' and Jesus said to Bartimaeus, 'Your faith has healed you.'

So is their trouble their lack of faith? Some would say 'Yes'. But that is a hopeless answer which gives the sufferer a deep sense of guilt. When the answer to our prayers is 'No', then the way to pray is to tell God of our pain, our desolation and our deep disappointment. Then God in Christ, who knew the deepest dereliction of the human spirit in the agony of the cross, will be there for us, and with us. He knows what it is not to know the answers: 'My God, my God, why...?

The only perfect priest

Every high priest is chosen from his fellow-men and appointed to serve God on their behalf, to offer sacrifices and offerings for sins. Since he himself is weak in many ways, he is able to be gentle with those who are ignorant and make mistakes. And because he is himself weak, he must offer sacrifices not only for the sins of the people but also for his own sins.

The high priest who went into the presence of God on behalf of the people in the Old Testament was a sinner. He stood in the presence of God to represent men and women as they are. Because he was weak like the rest of humankind he could be sympathetic to their weaknesses and to their sins. He knew what sin was like because he himself sinned. He was one of them—one of us. But he needed to be forgiven as well—and the fact that he was a sinner detracted from the effectiveness of his intercessory work.

Sin spoils things. It spoils relationships, and it is always a failure in love. Anyone who is in the business of helping other people, whether professionally or simply as a friend, knows that some people seem to be much harder to deal with than others. It is often our own hang-ups and sins (and our failure to have dealt with our own weakness) which hinder our helping. If someone comes to us in real emotional pain because the person whom they love has rejected them, we shall not be able to help them very much if what their story does is to make the unhealed pain of a rejection we have experienced well up and flood our consciousness with sadness and even resentment. The writer to the Hebrews is telling us about the weakness and sins of the Jewish high priest in order to show us how much better Jesus is at the job. Nothing we bring to him will ever perturb him...

A prayer

Lord Jesus Christ, help me to know with total confidence that there is nothing that I have ever done, or can do, which will mean that you cannot function as my high priest... bringing me to God... bringing God to me... forgiving all the sins I confess to you... and loving me for ever and ever.

No more decency

Blessed be the God and Father of our Lord Jesus Christ! By his great mercy we have been born anew to a living hope through the resurrection of Jesus Christ from the dead, and to an inheritance which is imperishable, undefiled, and unfading, kept in heaven for you, who by God's power are guarded through faith for a salvation ready to be revealed in the last time.

In our western world death is something that we hide behind the closed door of a refrigerator. We never see the decay and decomposition of a dead body. In the ancient world the unacceptable fact of death could not be hidden. 'He will be stinking by now,' they said to Jesus when he told them to roll away the stone from the front of Lazarus' grave. He wasn't stinking, because Jesus had called him forth from the grave to live again, and he walked out swathed in his grave clothes. But one day he would die again, and his body would go through the processes of decay that all bodies are subject to.

One day we shall all have to walk into the valley of the shadow of death. But it will make all the difference in the world if we know that the Lord who conquered death is our shepherd. It is far better for us than it was for the Jews. Later on in their history they had started to believe in the resurrection of the dead—and out of the depths of despair Job had cried out in faith that one day it was going to happen: 'I know that my Redeemer liveth, and that in my flesh shall I see God.' But the rest of the ancient world was without hope, and death was the end.

Into that desolation the Christian hope of eternal life shone like a great light in the darkness. A Christian had a new relationship with the living God and Father of our Lord Jesus Christ, and because of the resurrection he (and she—because women had a new status because of Christianity) had a new and living hope. The body would die, but it would be raised up to an endless life, imperishable and incorruptible.

A prayer

Thank you so much, Lord Jesus Christ, for the difference that your death makes to mine.

The
LOVE
of
GOD

The light of God

For God so loved the world that he gave his only Son, that whoever believes in him should not perish but have eternal life. For God sent the Son into the world, not to condemn the world, but that the world might be saved through him. He who believes in him is not condemned; he who does not believe is condemned already, because he has not believed in the name of the only Son of God. And this is the judgment, that the light has come into the world, and men loved darkness rather than light, because their deeds were evil. For every one who does evil hates the light, and does not come to the light, lest his deeds should be exposed. But he who does what is true comes to the light, that it may be clearly seen that his deeds have been wrought in God.

When my friends come to supper I light my room with the soft glow of candlelight, backed up by the low light of 25-watt bulbs in table lamps. Everything looks beautiful (even us!) because candlelight is a gentle light.

But when I want to clean my house I draw the curtains right back and let the light of day shine into all the hidden places: the corners where the spiders have made their webs and the places under furniture where I discover peanuts and paper-clips.

We see how things really are in a clear, bright light—not in a dim light or in the darkness. So what happens when we come into the light of God? Well, we see ourselves as we really are. We see that we're not very good at loving, even the people we love most, and that we are not what we should be. But we also begin to see God as he really is. It starts to dawn on us, like the warmth of the sun's rising, that the light shining into our hearts is the light of love. And just as I let the light of day shine into my room when I want to clean it, so does God shine his light into our hearts. He cleans them by forgiving our sins, and then comes and lives in them. So long as we'll come to the light and let him do it.

A prayer

Eternal Light, shine into my heart and let me see myself. Then let me see your glory shining in the face of Jesus Christ.

I love you

But now thus says the Lord, he who created you, O Jacob, he who formed you,
O Israel: Do not fear, for I have redeemed you; I have called you by name, you are
mine. When you pass through the waters, I will be with you; and through the rivers,
they shall not overwhelm you; when you walk through fire you shall not be burned,
and the flame shall not consume you. For I am the Lord your God, the Holy One of
Israel, your Saviour. I give Egypt as your ransom, Ethiopia and Seba in exchange
for you. Because you are precious in my sight, and honoured, and I love you, I give
people in return for you, nations in exchange for your life.

Sometimes I use this whole passage when I am taking a meditation—and I ask people to put their own names instead of Jacob and Israel. A theology student raised a mild objection once, saying he didn't think we were entitled to do that. But I believe that we are—because in a sense each one of us, if we are Christian believers, are members of the family of faith of which Abraham, Isaac and Jacob were the founding fathers—the beginning of the people of God—people who have seen something of the glory of God, and trust and worship him. The glory of God is his nature—and the believer knows that God is merciful, loving and just, and he is a God who forgives sinners. It says in Exodus 33:11 that God talked to Moses face to face, as a man speaks to his friend—and the New Testament says that Jesus was the friend of publicans and sinners. God shows the world the vastness of his love by loving one small and rather tiresome nation who were continually unfaithful and disobedient, and who wanted to do their own will instead of God's. But to some extent or other we are all like that—so that Israel can stand for all of us, and for me in particular. And it wasn't Egypt, Ethiopia and Seba that God gave as our ransom. It was his Son.

A way to pray

Read out the passage, and put in your name instead of Jacob—and 'my son' or
'my daughter' for Israel. We are the sons and daughters of the living God, and by
faith we are related to Israel and to Abraham. As you read, think of the waters that
you are going through right now. As you read of the fire, remember that our God is a
consuming fire—but know that because you are loved, forgiven and redeemed you will
not be burned. Think of your great preciousness to God—and when you have finished
be silent for a few moments, in thankfulness.

Consequences

'Therefore wait for me,' says the Lord, '...For my decision is to gather nations, to assemble kingdoms, to pour out upon them my indignation, all the heat of my anger; for in the fire of my passion all the earth shall be consumed. At that time I will change the speech of the peoples to a pure speech, that all of them may call on the name of the Lord and serve him with one accord... On that day you shall not be put to shame because of all the deeds by which you have rebelled against me; for then I will remove from your midst your proudly exultant ones, and you shall no longer be haughty in my holy mountain. For I will leave in the midst of you a people humble and lowly. They shall seek refuge in the name of the Lord—the remnant of Israel; they shall do no wrong and utter no lies, nor shall a deceitful tongue be found in their mouths. Then they will pasture and lie down and no one shall make them afraid.'

The whole purpose of the fire of God's wrath is to purify the people whom he loves—and he loves the whole world.

'If you don't stop doing that,' a provoked and angry parent will say to a teenager who is acting destructively, 'then I shall do that...' Often the parent doesn't carry out the threat; and anyway, to solve the problem of what is the right sort of discipline needs the wisdom of Solomon (which we are in fact promised, if we only ask for it).

But God doesn't make idle threats. As 2 Peter 3:9 says, God is waiting and being patient, 'not willing that any should perish but that all should come to repentance.'

The judgments of God are happening all the time—as individuals and societies break up and break down and fall apart because they break the laws of the God of love. It is as if judgment is programmed into things—so that when people act corruptly and destructively their own evil results in their own corruption and destruction. They become corrupt people—and that in itself is the real punishment: to be a destructive, unkind person rather than a creative, loving person, being recreated in the image and likeness of God, who is both creator and lover. We need to be being made Christ-like, not proud and self-willed, going our own way, but obedient and gentle; like the Son of God, who said 'I am meek and lowly in heart' (Matthew 11:29).

Think

Why is it the meek and not the proud who will inherit the earth?

The one great sacrifice

*As the Father has loved me, so have I loved you; abide in my love. If you keep
my commandments, you will abide in my love, just as I have kept my Father's
commandments and abide in his love. These things I have spoken to you, that my joy
may be in you, and that your joy may be full. This is my commandment, that you
love one another as I have loved you. Greater love has no man than this, that a man
lay down his life for his friends.*

When I first became a Christian I was rather condemning of anything in the
Church which I considered less than totally doctrinally sound. Thankfully
I have mellowed a bit since then, though I still refuse to say or sing anything in a service which I think is false. One of my favourite songs is 'Jesus,
we celebrate your victory' by John Gibson, and I sing it with great delight
and gusto. But for one line I clamp my mouth tight shut: 'And in his presence, our problems disappear.' They don't! They really don't. And if we
tell people they do then they are going to be desperately disappointed.

In my condemning days a hymn I refused to sing was 'O valiant hearts'.
I loved the picture but I was uneasy about the truth: 'And through the veil,
the Victor's pitying eyes look down to bless our lesser Calvaries.' But there
is no other Calvary than his, I would anguish. Christ died once—for all.
But now I understand a bit more. A man dying in a battle... a woman dying
from a bomb... they are in their way 'lesser Calvaries'. They are in their
own way laying down their lives for their friends, and for their country,
even if they barely understand what the fighting is about. And perhaps at
the end they lift up their eyes and look at Jesus dying on his Calvary, and
understand why he died.

A prayer

*Hold thou thy cross before my closing eyes,
Shine through the gloom, and point me to the skies.
Heaven's morning breaks, and earth's vain shadows flee.
In life, in death, O Lord, abide with me.*

Henry Francis Lyte

Judgment, love and freedom

'The nations must get ready and come to the Valley of Judgment. There I, the Lord, will sit to judge all the surrounding nations. They are very wicked; cut them down like corn at harvest time; crush them as grapes are crushed in a full winepress until the wine runs over.' Thousands and thousands are in the Valley of Judgment. It is there that the day of the Lord will soon come. The sun and the moon grow dark, and the stars no longer shine.

'Your will be done,' Jesus told us to pray—and if the will of God was always done then Jesus would have been wasting his words to say what he did and we would be wasting our time to pray as he told us.

'It is not his will that any should be lost, but that all should come to repentance,' it says in 2 Peter 3:9 (REB)—but before that the writer says that some will be lost, because not all will come to repentance. 'By God's will the present heavens and earth are being reserved for burning; they are being kept until the day of judgment when the godless will be destroyed.'

The will of God is that the godless should repent, and be godly, and be forgiven, and be loved. The will of God is that they should be redeemed, and live with him for ever in the glory of heaven. But the will of God is not always done—since he has created the human race with free will: to accept his love and forgiveness and to say 'Yes' to God, or to reject his love, refuse forgiveness, and say 'No' to God. Even God cannot *make* people love him.

We don't like the idea of judgment, or the thought that some people in the world will be lost and cast into what Jesus described as 'the outer darkness'. But not liking something, or not believing something, doesn't mean that it won't happen. We can be wrong—and we can't say that we haven't been warned.

To think about

Think about the day of the Lord and the day of judgment. Think about the one who will be our judge. Think about Jesus weeping over Jerusalem. Think about the will of God. Think about the love of God.

Purity of heart

*How great is the love that the Father has shown us! We were called God's children,
and such we are; and the reason why the godless world does not recognize us is that it
has not known him. Here and now, dear friends, we are God's children; what we shall
be has not yet been disclosed, but we know that when it is disclosed we shall be like
him, because we shall see him as he is. Everyone who has this hope before him purifies
himself, as Christ is pure.*

Today I was talking with someone whose life is going through a profound
change. Metamorphosis was the word he used to describe it. It wasn't
comfortable for him, and as we talked we wondered what it was like for
the dragonfly nymph when the day came for it to change its form. We were
well aware that the dragonfly doesn't have a human consciousness, and
we were using it as a symbol to stand for the profound and radical changes
that take place in our human lives. And the most dramatic change of all
will be when we see Christ face to face and are finally transformed to be
like him.

That's what we hope for—in the Christian meaning of hope: which
isn't 'Oh dear, I do hope the milk hasn't gone sour' when it is past its sell-
by date and almost certainly has. It's the hope that we hear about in the
Prayer Book service for the Burial of the Dead at the committal: 'we therefore commit his body to the ground; earth to earth, ashes to ashes, dust to
dust; in sure and certain hope of the Resurrection to eternal life, through
our Lord Jesus Christ...'

So if we have that hope, then what? John says that we purify ourselves.
But what does that mean, and what are we to do? In the last century the
Danish theologian Søren Kierkegaard wrote a book entitled *Purity of
Heart is to will one thing*. He subtitled it 'Spiritual preparation for the
office of confession'—but it has a great deal to teach every Christian, even
those who do not have formal confession as part of their spiritual discipline.

The 'one thing' we have to do is to will the will of God. It's what Jesus
prayed in the garden of Gethsemane: 'My Father, if it is possible, may this
cup be taken from me. Yet not as I will, but as you will' (Matthew 26:39,
NIV).

Tell me the old, old story

The people came up out of the Jordan on the tenth day of the first month, and they camped in Gilgal on the east border of Jericho. Those twelve stones, which they had taken out of the Jordan, Joshua set up in Gilgal, saying to the Israelites, 'When your children ask their parents in time to come, "What do these stones mean?" then you shall let your children know, "Israel crossed over the Jordan here on dry ground." For the Lord your God dried up the waters of the Jordan for you until you crossed over, as the Lord your God did to the Red Sea, which he dried up for us until we crossed over, so that all the peoples of the earth may know that the hand of the Lord is mighty, and so that you may fear the Lord your God forever.'

The account of the twelve stones being taken out of the Jordan comes in chapter 3. They were to be a memorial and a reminder—for Israel to remember in the future what God had done in the past. We need to remember both our personal history and the history of our nation. In the future Israel would fall away from her high calling as the people of God— even though the calling and the purpose of God would always remain the same. Israel would fall away over and over again—just as we do. And all the time God remains faithful. Waiting for us to turn back to him again— and encountering us through everything that happens in our lives in order to persuade us to do so. He won't ever force us—but he will for ever be wooing us and calling to us.

The Israelites were told to tell their children the story of what had happened—and to keep on telling them through the years. Children love stories—and so do most grown-ups. But somewhere along the line we haven't told our children the Christian story very effectively. Recently some young people were asked what the Ten Commandments were. Between them all they managed to scrape up two—the seventh, about adultery, being one of them. They knew nothing of the wonder of the love of God, or the amazing events of Good Friday, Easter Day and the coming of the Holy Spirit at Pentecost.

A prayer

'Tell me the old, old story, of Jesus and his love'—and then let me tell it to other people and to the children of our nation.

I am the light

*Again Jesus spoke to them, saying, 'I am the light of the world; he who follows me will
not walk in darkness, but will have the light of life.'*

Jesus is speaking to the Pharisees. They were like the people in our reading yesterday, who loved darkness rather than light, because their deeds
were evil. They hated the light—and in the darkness of a Friday morning
they put it out. But in the glory of Easter morning the light shone out
again—and the risen Christ appeared to his astonished, terrified and
delighted followers.

He doesn't appear to us in the same way. But he still calls us to follow
him, and he still makes the same promises.

You probably know Holman Hunt's painting 'The Light of the World'.
Christ is standing outside a house and knocking on the door. There is no
handle on the outside, because if Christ is to go inside the owner of the
house will have to open the door and invite him in.

Years ago, when my life was in a dreadful mess and I was deeply unhappy, a curate called John Collins told me about that picture. He said that
if I would ask Christ into my heart he would change my life and forgive my
sins. So I went home, knelt by my bed, and read out the verse John had
given me: 'Behold, I stand at the door and knock; if any one hears my
voice and opens the door, I will come in to him and eat with him, and he
with me' (Revelation 3:20). Then I prayed, 'Lord, I open the door of my
heart now. Please come in.'

I know that he did, because I knew then (with a deep certainty that
nothing has ever been able to shake) that God is my Father, that he loves
me, and that my sins are forgiven. I have sometimes prayed the prayer
since—asking Christ to enter rooms in the house of my life that I had kept
locked. But that first prayer totally changed my life.

A way to pray

*Sit in silence and let the light of Christ shine into your heart—and into every room
in the house of your life. Then, if you are willing, invite him to come in—perhaps for
the first time, or perhaps into places where you have never allowed him before.*

With laughter

When the Lord restored the fortunes of Zion, we were like those who dream. Then our mouth was filled with laughter, and our tongue with shouts of joy; then they said among the nations, 'The Lord has done great things for them.' The Lord has done great things for us; we are glad. Restore our fortunes, O Lord, like the watercourses in the Negeb! May those who sow in tears reap with shouts of joy! He that goes forth weeping, bearing the seed for sowing, shall come home with shouts of joy, bringing his sheaves with him.

Sometimes we think that God is someone we only turn to in times of trouble. When we get it hopelessly wrong we see him, as C.S. Lewis put it, as a sort of parachute for use in an emergency. But when our relationship with God is as it is meant to be, it is a life spent in continual communion— enjoying each other's presence. (Do we dare to believe that God enjoys ours? It says he does… that 'the Lord delights in his people—Psalm 149:4). Then everything that we do, and all the emotions that we experience, happen in the presence of the God who lives within us through his Spirit.

So our joy and our laughter are ways to speak to God just as much as our tears, our groans, our complaints and our intercessions. Perhaps part of the joy in the laughter comes from the release of tension. The great dramatists knew how to relieve our pain in their tragedies… they suddenly give us the comic relief of laughter. Perhaps our own ability to laugh at ourselves is a way of inner release and of growing towards wholeness. My father could never laugh at himself until he was 65, when he became a Christian. Then he began to see the funny side of himself. He even enjoyed it when we laughed at him, in great love and delight at his silliness in some of the things he did.

A prayer

Thank you for laughter, Lord. Thank you for the release that it gives. Help me to laugh at myself, and at other people… but tenderly, and in love.

God's waiting and ours

Yet the Lord is waiting to show you his favour, yet he yearns to have pity on you; for the Lord is a God of justice. Happy are all who wait for him! O people of Zion who dwell in Jerusalem, you shall weep no more. The Lord will show you favour and answer you when he hears your cry for help. The Lord may give you bread of adversity and water of affliction, but he who teaches you shall no longer be hidden out of sight, but with your own eyes you shall see him always. If you stray from the road to right or left you shall hear with your own ears a voice behind you saying, This is the way; follow it.

God is waiting for us—and if we wait on him we shall be happy. Our waiting is not a passive thing sitting down and waiting doubtfully to see if something will happen. It is a positive, prayerful waiting, knowing that something will definitely happen—although it may not be what we expect. God is waiting with eager longing to bless us—but we have to want the blessing. Perhaps we are in the far country, like the prodigal son. Perhaps we are feeling very sad about something, and feeling hopeless. Perhaps every day is such a struggle that we hardly know how to swallow the bread of adversity that is on our plate—and perhaps we are almost drowned with our sorrows.

Whatever our circumstances, our Creator God who loves us is longing to bless us—and our task is to wait on him in prayer and in hope. We can cry out for help as loudly as we like. It isn't that we need to shout to make him hear—but sometimes shouting (or weeping) can be a way to express our pain. Then the promise—of the presence of God with us all along life's way, and a promise of the guidance of God when we step out of the way. A voice in our ears that we know and recognize—the voice of the good shepherd speaking to the sheep who has strayed away from him, or who is simply a very sad and suffering sheep in need of comfort: 'My sheep hear my voice, and I know them, and they follow me; and I shall give them eternal life, and they shall never perish, and no one shall snatch them out of my hand' (John 10:27, 28).

We will come to you

'Whoever accepts my commands and obeys them is the one who loves me. My Father will love whoever loves me; I too will love him and reveal myself to him.' Judas (not Judas Iscariot) said, 'Lord, how can it be that you will reveal yourself to us and not to the world?' Jesus answered him, 'Whoever loves me will obey my teaching. My Father will love him, and my Father and I will come to him and live with him. Whoever does not love me does not obey my teaching. And the teaching you have heard is not mine, but comes from the Father, who sent me.'

Was Jesus saying that before either he or his Father will love us we have to do just what he tells us and also to love him? If he was then the gospel isn't good news. It's bad. Because we'll never manage either the living or the loving on our own. In his brilliant commentary on John's Gospel, William Temple helps us to understand what this difficult passage really means:

'The Father loves all his children with an infinite love, such love as could be expressed only by giving His only-begotten Son. Yet there is a special love also in His heart for those who love that Son. The universal love of God is not a featureless uniformity of good-will. Good-will to all there is; but also for each whatever special quality of love is appropriate to him; and there must be a special quality of love for those who love the Son whom the Father loved before the foundation of the world. The Son Himself, who is the "express image" of the Father's universal love, has a special quality of love (how could it be otherwise?) for those who love Him in return; and to them He will manifest Himself.' (*Readings in St John's Gospel*, Macmillan, 1959)

A prayer

Lord God, I thank you for this amazing truth—that you will make your home in my heart: you who created the galaxies, and our world, and me... you who are Father, Son and Holy Spirit, Creator and Lover.

A gift of love

Yet it was kind of you to share my trouble. And you Philippians yourselves know
that in the beginning of the gospel, when I left Macedonia, no church entered into
partnership with me in giving and receiving except you only; for even in Thessalonica
you sent me help once and again.

It was because Christ was in him that Paul could handle being either rich
or poor. He was totally content with either state. He didn't need anything,
because of the deep delight and satisfaction that his relationship with
Christ gave to him. But he was delighted that the Philippians had cared so
much for his welfare and well-being that they had sent Epaphroditus to
him with their gifts, and the reason for his delight and his rejoicing was
that it showed him the quality of their Christian lives. It is God-like to
give—and meanness and tight-fistedness can never flow from the love of
God. Jesus spoke of giving a good measure that was pressed down and
'running over' (Luke 6:38)—and when someone gives to us like that, out
of their love and affection for us, it warms our heart, even if we don't in
the strictest sense 'need' their gift. That's how it was for Paul.

The 'fruit' that Paul longed to see growing in his converts was the fruit
of the Spirit: 'Love, joy, peace, patience, kindness, goodness, faithfulness,
gentleness and self control' (Galatians 5:22, 23). Every year an old apple
tree in my garden bears a heavy crop of red apples, with a sweet smell and
a lovely flavour, crunchy and juicy—and every time I go past the tree I
can't resist picking one and eating it (and the same goes for my friends).
My apple tree bears apples like that because that's the sort of tree it is—
and the Christians in Philippi sent their gift to Paul out of the love of their
hearts, because that's the sort of people they were. Christians with a generous heart of love, like the heart of God.

A reflection

Think of sweet, ripe apples on a tree, warm with the autumn sunshine, fragrant and
juicy. Think of your own giving to your friends and your family, and to your church
and to the needs of the hungry world. Think of the self-giving love of God...

The God who comes to us

Comfort, O comfort my people, says your God. Speak tenderly to Jerusalem, and cry to her that she has served her term, that her penalty is paid, that she has received from the Lord's hand double for all her sins. A voice cries out: 'In the wilderness prepare the way of the Lord, make straight in the desert a highway for our God. Every valley shall be lifted up, and every mountain and hill be made low; the uneven ground shall become level, and the rough places a plain. Then the glory of the Lord shall be revealed, and all people shall see it together, for the mouth of the Lord has spoken.'

The people of God had been suffering because they had been sinning—and the basis of their sin was a breaking of their relationship with the God who was their divine husband. Israel was a faithless wife who had committed adultery—and God had sent her into exile and into the wilderness to woo her back again. Someone once said that there is no such thing as sin. There are only sinners—human beings who fail in one way or another to love God and to love other people. Sinning always has that failure of love at its root. All that differs is the degree—as Jesus made so plain in the Sermon on the Mount: 'You have heard that it was said, "You shall not commit adultery." But I say to you that everyone who looks at a woman with lust has already committed adultery with her in his heart' (Matthew 5:27–28).

But God the divine husband never stops loving his wife, even when she is faithless, and he never stops loving his world. The good news that Isaiah cries out to comfort people in their sorrow is that God himself will come to them. Mark uses these words from Isaiah to begin his Gospel: 'The beginning of the good news of the Jesus Christ, the Son of God. As it is written in the prophet Isaiah, "See, I am sending my messenger ahead of you, who will prepare your way; the voice of one crying out in the wilderness, 'Prepare the way of the Lord, make his paths straight.'"' The one who cries out in the wilderness is John the Baptist. The Lord who comes is Jesus.

A way to pray

Think about your own problems and sorrows. Then imagine Jesus the Lord entering into your situation. Talk to him and listen to him. Then do the same for the situation of another person or group of people.

Born for love

Having purified your souls by your obedience to the truth for a sincere love of the brethren, love one another earnestly from the heart. You have been born anew, not of perishable seed but of imperishable, through the living and abiding word of God; for 'All flesh is like grass and all its glory like the flower of grass. The grass withers, and the flower falls, but the word of the Lord abides for ever.' That word is the good news which was preached to you. So put away all malice and all guile and insincerity and envy and all slander. Like newborn babes, long for the pure spiritual milk, that by it you may grow up to salvation; for you have tasted the kindness of the Lord.

All creatures have the same nature as their parents, whether the creature is a tiny blackbird chick just hatched out of a turquoise spotted egg, or a foal that stands on its legs and nuzzles its mother only minutes after it is born; or a human baby, totally dependent for life on another human being. Christians, born again of the Spirit of God, have the nature of God. And the nature of God is love. It is impossible for a real Christian not to love, because the new nature growing within her (or him) is the same as God's nature. But the new nature has to grow, just as a baby has. The newborn Christian is to thirst for the pure spiritual milk of the 'word'. That isn't just the Bible. It is all things that have to do with the Word, who is God himself. The Word that went forth from God on the first day of creation... the Word who was 'in the beginning with God'... the Word that the whole of creation declares about the glory of God without even speaking a word. The word of the Lord abides for ever—and it is through that word that the Christian is born.

A prayer

Living Lord God, help me to nourish your life in me—and to thirst for all things that flow from you, the living word. Help me to live—to love you and my neighbour and myself, with the love that flows from your heart of love.

Love letters

Are we beginning to praise ourselves again? Some people need letters that speak well of them. Do we need those kinds of letters, either to you or from you? You ourselves are our letter. You are written on our hearts. Everyone knows you and reads you. You make it clear that you are a letter from Christ. You are the result of our work for God. You are a letter written not with ink but with the Spirit of the living God. You are a letter written not on tablets made out of stone but on human hearts. Through Christ, we can be sure of this because of our faith in God's power. In ourselves we are not able to claim anything for ourselves. The power to do what we do comes from God. He has given us the power to serve under a new covenant. The covenant is not based on the written Law of Moses. It comes from the Holy Spirit.

'Love letters straight from my heart' is the first line of an old popular song, and the letters that Paul is writing about are really love letters. He has got a good metaphor, and he uses it in two ways.

These Corinthian Christians whom he loves so much (and whom because of his love he disciplined so severely) are a letter written on his heart (by Christ) for him to read—and they are also letters written by the living God for other people to read. They are love letters, because the Spirit of the living God sheds abroad in our hearts the love which God has for us.

'We love [God] because he first loved us,' says 1 John 4:19; it goes on to say that the test of our love for God is that it spills over in love for other people. We love them with the overflow and the overspill of the love that is poured into our hearts when we are loved. When we know that we are loved, and are ourselves loving in response, then it shows. People can see it in our faces—and as we look at them they will see something of the love of God for them in our eyes, as well as our love for them.

To think about

Since you are a letter from the living, loving God to all the people living around you, what are they reading?

The father's sorrow

When Israel was a child I loved him, and I called my son out of Egypt. But the more I called, the further they went away from me; they offered sacrifice to Baal and burnt incense to idols. I myself taught Ephraim to walk, I myself took them by the arm, but they did not know that I was the one caring for them, that I was leading them with human ties, with leading-strings of love, that, with them, I was like someone lifting an infant to his cheek, and that I bent down to feed him.

One human relationship is not enough to show us how God loves us. The love between a husband and a wife shows us something of the love. The love of a father for his son shows us something else—and there is heartache in both the loves. This son has gone away from the father, just as the prodigal son went away. Hosea tells us what goes on in the father's heart as he yearns for his son. He remembers when his son was a little boy, just out of babyhood and learning to walk. The father helped him—probably proud of his first, wobbling steps. He put a leading string on him—to lead him in love along the right way. He picked him up to cuddle him and bent down to feed him. That is what God did for Israel—but Israel didn't know who was looking after him.

To think about

Do I realize how God has looked after me and led me all the days of my life—except when I have turned away into my own way? Is God yearning after me because I have gone away from him? Am I like the eldest son in the story of the waiting father, living in the father's house but not enjoying the father's presence and all the benefits? Or have I come home to the Father—and has he made his home in me? Jesus said, 'If a man loves me, he will keep my word, and my Father will love him, and we will come to him and make our home with him' (John 14:23).

The bent and beloved world

Do all things without grumbling or questioning, that you may be blameless and innocent, children of God without blemish in the midst of a crooked and perverse generation, among whom you shine as lights in the world, holding fast the word of life, so that in the day of Christ I may be proud that I did not run in vain or labour in vain. Even if I am to be poured as a libation upon the sacrificial offering of your faith, I am glad and rejoice with you all. Likewise you also should be glad and rejoice with me.

Some people are always grumbling and criticizing. Nothing and no one ever seems to be right—and they put themselves up by putting other people down. 'Don't be like that,' says Paul to the Philippians (and through them to us). You are the children of God (and once we know that glory we should never need to put anyone down to put ourselves up). So be what you are—the light of the world. Jesus said that he was and that we are too: 'You are the light of the world... Let your light so shine before men that they may see your good works and give glory to your Father who is in heaven' (Matthew 5:14, 16).

Paul takes up the same idea, and speaks of shining as lights in the world 'in the midst of a crooked and perverse generation'. But God still loves crooked and perverse generations and crooked and perverse people, and he wants to straighten out their crookedness and bring their perverseness into line with his loving will for them. Christians are called to be part of the healing process. To straighten out God's beloved world. To lighten its darkness. And to offer it the word of life that Christ died to speak. And Paul was happy to die, like a cup of wine poured out as a libation on the offering of the Christian's sacrificial faith.

A prayer

Lord Jesus Christ, light of the world, shine into me and out of me, with your healing light, and lead me to the people you love so that I can hold out to them the word of life.

Love!

One of the teachers of the law came and heard them debating. Noticing that Jesus had given them a good answer, he asked him, 'Of all the commandments, which is the most important?' 'The most important one,' answered Jesus, 'is this: "Hear, O Israel, the Lord our God, the Lord is one. Love the Lord your God with all your heart and with all your soul and with all your mind and with all your strength." The second is this: "Love your neighbour as yourself." There is no commandment greater than these.'

They weren't new, these two commandments that Jesus said were the greatest. They were there right back in the Pentateuch (Deuteronomy 6:4, 5 and Leviticus 19:18 if you want to look them up). 'Love your neighbour as yourself...' isn't about a narcissistic self-love but about a healthy self-love. If we are hungry we will feed ourselves, and if we are thirsty we will get ourselves something to drink. That is the most basic love of all—and when we dare to find out who is hungry and who is thirsty we shall probably ask the question that produced the story of the Good Samaritan: 'Lord, who is my neighbour?' And we might like the answer as little as Jesus' listeners when he gave it.

But what about the commandment to love God? What does that really mean and how do we do it? To love with all our heart means to love with the whole of our being. To love with all our understanding means to use and exercise our mind and our thinking in the process. And to love with all our strength means to bend all our energy to our loving. But what does it mean to love? Love is not an emotion and not a feeling of delight or rapture (though sometimes that can be the result of loving). To love God is quite simply to do the will of God. Jesus said in the Gospel of John, 'If you love me, keep my commandments.' We use our heart in commitment to them—our mind in discovering and exploring them—and the whole of our strength in performing them.

Move with the Spirit

*'At that very moment three men who had been sent to me from Caesarea arrived at the
house where I was staying. The Spirit told me to go with them without hesitation.
These six fellow-believers from Joppa accompanied me to Caesarea, and we all went
into the house of Cornelius. He told us how he had seen an angel standing in his
house, who said to him, "Send someone to Joppa for a man whose full name is Simon
Peter. He will speak words to you by which you and all your family will be saved."
And when I began to speak, the Holy Spirit came down on them just as on us at the
beginning. Then I remembered what the Lord had said: "John baptized with water, but
you will be baptized with the Holy Spirit." It is clear that God gave those Gentiles
the same gift that he gave us when we believed in the Lord Jesus Christ; who was I,
then, to try to stop God?'*

The living God is always pouring out his love and himself into improper
places and improper people—and the rigidly religious find it disturbing
and upsetting. They would prefer God to behave like a tidy canal, staying
within the banks which they have dug, and directed where they have chosen. But instead the river of life flows just where it chooses. It floods its
banks in glorious abandon and abundance, and the desolate deserts of the
earth start to blossom and bear fruit. Isaiah prophesies that one day, 'The
earth shall be filled with the knowledge of the Lord as the waters cover the
sea' (11:9), and in 49:6 of the same book God speaking through Isaiah
says, 'It is too light a thing that you should be my servant to raise up the
tribes of Jacob... I will give you as a light to the nations, that my salvation
may reach to the end of the earth'. Now it was happening. God was giving
himself to Gentiles as well as to Jews—and not doing it in the proper
order! Pouring out himself in the baptism of the Spirit *before* they had
gone through the procedures—and doing it even as Peter was in the
process of preaching. First the baptism of the Holy Spirit—and then the
baptism of water. You can read all about it in Acts 10.

God's point of view

Sing, O Daughter of Zion; shout aloud, O Israel! ... The Lord has taken away your punishment, he has turned back your enemy. The Lord, the King of Israel, is with you; never again will you fear any harm. On that day they will say to Jerusalem, 'Do not fear, O Zion; do not let your hands hang limp. The Lord your God is with you, he is mighty to save. He will take great delight in you, he will quiet you with his love, he will rejoice over you with singing.'

All the anger and the wrath of the God of love has one great purpose: to win the love of his beloved and to be loved in return. This is what God has always wanted and always will. We see God in Hosea as an anguished, angry and jealous husband, longing for his adulterous (but still beloved) wife to come back to him, and we see him taking action to win her back to him again.

God is the lover and the husband of his people. But we need to consider all our human loves in order to comprehend more fully the wonder and the glory of the love of God.

God is our friend. The Lord 'used to speak to Moses face to face, as a man speaks to his friend,' says Exodus 33:11; and Jesus says to his disciples that 'you are my friends if you do what I command you. No longer do I call you servants, for the servant does not know what his master is doing; but I have called you friends' (John 15:14–15).

God comforts us like a mother, says Isaiah 66:13; and God is our Father. Jesus tells us about the nature of God by telling us the story of the prodigal son and the waiting father, running out to welcome his son home with his arms wide open to embrace him. Jesus shows us the depth of that love by dying for us—and one of the eucharistic prayers in the *Alternative Service Book* says that 'he opened wide his arms for us on the cross'.

He opened them wide for us, and died for us, because he wants to hold us and embrace us in his love—like a mother, a father, a lover...

Reflect

Spend some time reflecting on God's love and longing for you—and consider the whole business of salvation from his point of view instead of your own.

Troubling words

In the sixth month the angel Gabriel was sent from God to a city of Galilee named
Nazareth, to a virgin betrothed to a man whose name was Joseph, of the house of
David; and the virgin's name was Mary. And he came to her and said, 'Hail, O
favoured one, the Lord is with you!' But she was greatly troubled at the saying, and
considered in her mind what sort of greeting this might be. And the angel said to her,
'Do not be afraid, Mary, for you have found favour with God.'

There has been controversial talk about the birth of Jesus ever since it happened. There was then and there is now. But those who find the virgin
birth hard to believe in do not need to despair of their Christian faith. Our
salvation does not depend on our belief in this doctrine. It depends on
our belief and trust in the forgiveness of God through the death of Christ:
on the belief that 'God so loved the world that he gave his only Son, that
whoever believes in him should not perish but have everlasting life' (John
3:16). But even for those who find this particular belief difficult it has
something very powerful to say. So, whenever you listen to the Christmas
story, will you pray that God will speak to your heart through it and reveal
his glory to you?

Those who do believe that the birth of Jesus happened just as it says
still need to pray just the same prayer. Because we are not finished with
the story simply because we believe it. We have to let it speak to us in our
condition and affect our life and our world.

When God speaks to our world he always speaks to a person—and
what he says is often disturbing and awkward. That was true for Mary and
it will be true for us.

To think about

What must it have been like for Mary, a girl in her teens, to have a sudden and
powerful message from God? What would you feel if God came to you in power, to
fulfil some purpose that he had for you? What if it disturbed your whole life? Think
of Mary's openness to the start of the message . . . and of her dread.

Renewed and restored

'Be glad, people of Zion, rejoice at what the Lord your God has done for you. He has
given you the right amount of autumn rain; he has poured down the winter rain for
you and the spring rain as before. The threshing-places will be full of corn; the pits
beside the presses will overflow with wine and olive oil. I will give you back what you
lost in the years when swarms of locusts ate your crops. It was I who sent this army
against you. Now you will have plenty to eat, and be satisfied. You will praise the
Lord your God, who has done wonderful things for you. My people will never be
despised again. Then, Israel, you will know that I am among you, and that I, the
Lord, am your God and there is no other.'

I moved to Oxford during a heatwave and a drought. Port Meadow, the
local common land, is nearby, and the whole meadow was brown and
parched. The river was low, and the cows and horses that graze there had
no pasture. But now, after a week's rain, the grass is green again and the
animals are feeding again. The grass grows up from the roots, right at the
bottom of the plant—and spiritual growth always springs from the roots.
For the people of Zion the renewed rain was the outward sign of an inner
renewal of their fellowship with God, and the things that they had lost
were being restored to them.

For some of us the years in our past seemed to be wasted years. We
were separated and cut off from the love of God. Or we felt as if we were.
The reality was that the love was always there, pursuing us and wooing us,
but we had either separated ourselves from the relationship or else never
entered into it. Yet in the providence of God those years are not wasted.
He uses them in the making and remaking of us. When I first read 'I will
give you back the years which the locust has eaten' (RSV), I believed that
they were the words of God to me, and a promise of what he would do in
the future. And he has done for me just what the words say. Other people
I know have believed them in the same way and had the same experience.
In the providence of God nothing is wasted—and whatever happened in
our past can be used to enrich our present.

Reflect

Our spirits are dry because they forget to feed on you.

St John of the Cross

Put on love

As God's chosen ones, holy and beloved, clothe yourselves with compassion, kindness, humility, meekness, and patience. Bear with one another and, if anyone has a complaint against another, forgive each other; just as the Lord has forgiven you, so you also must forgive. Above all, clothe yourselves with love, which binds everything together in perfect harmony. And let the peace of Christ rule in your hearts, to which indeed you were called in the one body. And be thankful. Let the word of Christ dwell in you richly; teach and admonish one another in all wisdom; and with gratitude in your hearts sing psalms, hymns, and spiritual songs to God. And whatever you do, in word or deed, do everything in the name of the Lord Jesus, giving thanks to God the Father through him.

They are beautiful clothes that God wants us to wear. The garment that everyone will see first is love, because we put that on top of all the other qualities. We know the enormous difference between being with someone who loves us and someone who doesn't. The water lilies in my small pond only open out their petals when the sun is shining—and we only blossom fully as human beings when the light of love is shining on us.

The outside garment of love has other qualities within it and underneath it. If you have time, spend a few moments reading again the first sentence of the passage printed above, and reflecting on the meaning of the qualities Paul tells us to put on.

He also tells us to admonish one another—and to admonish means to exhort a person to do what he (or she) should do; to give advice; to warn about something; to inform, and to remind about something. The person who is being admonished doesn't always welcome it, but it is an important part of Christian living and growing. The details of what we are to admonish someone about are all there in the word of Christ. But we are never to take off that outer garment of love—so the person being admonished knows how much they are loved. If we have a problem with the loving, then we had better leave the admonishing to someone else.

A way to pray

Reflect on the qualities that we are to put on after we have taken the others off.

Luke 1:46–49 (RSV)

Revealing the glory

And Mary said, 'My soul magnifies the Lord, and my spirit rejoices in God my Saviour, for he has regarded the low estate of his handmaiden. For behold, henceforth all generations will call me blessed; for he who is mighty has done great things for me, and holy is his name.

I used to think that to magnify something simply meant to enlarge it so that it could be seen in more detail. So I found it puzzling that even such a specially chosen woman as Mary the mother of Jesus could 'magnify the Lord'. But the first meaning that the *Shorter Oxford Dictionary* gives of the verb 'to magnify' is 'to speak or act for the glory of (a person or thing); to laud, extol' (though those last two meanings are archaic). But the first definition made perfect sense. The whole of Mary's soul, which was her true self and her whole being, was both speaking and acting for the glory of God. Through what she said and what she did, the nature of God would be revealed far more clearly to the world than it had ever been revealed before.

God was going to come into his world through a woman—and women were not highly regarded in those days. (They are not *very* highly regarded in our day!) God was going to put down the mighty from their thrones and exalt those of low degree. The Son who was to be born to Mary would turn the world's values upside-down. He would be the friend of sinners (prostitutes and collaborators in the society of his day—I wonder who it would be in ours?) and teach that it was the meek who would inherit the earth—not the rich or the powerful.

Consider

For thus saith the high and lofty One, who inhabits eternity, whose name is Holy; I dwell in the high and holy place, and also with him who is of a contrite and humble spirit, to revive the spirit of the humble, and to revive the heart of the contrite. (Isaiah 57:15)

A new engagement

*I shall betroth you to myself for ever, I shall betroth you in uprightness and justice,
and faithful love and tenderness. Yes, I shall betroth you to myself in loyalty and in
the knowledge of Yahweh. When that day comes, I shall respond—declares Yahweh—
I shall respond to the heavens and they will respond to the earth and the earth will
respond to the grain, the new wine and oil, and they will respond to Jezreel. I shall
sow her in the country to be mine, I shall take pity on Lo-Ruhamah, I shall tell
Lo-Ammi, 'You are my people,' and he will say, 'You are my God.'*

God is making his plans for his beloved and now the transformation and
the turnabout is going to begin. A betrothal is where a marriage begins,
and God and his beloved are going to begin again. There will be the
delight of falling in love all over again (although God never fell out of love
even if Hosea did).

Now there will be a new start and a betrothal that will last for ever.

Someone I know became a Christian when he was middle-aged. He had
not been either a good father or a good husband. But his new relationship
with Christ transformed his other relationships and he would tell people
about the dramatic change in his life. 'I've fallen in love with my wife for
the first time,' he said. It was true.

When someone really knows the love of God, the blessings start to flow
out from their heart like a river. Even the earth knows the difference. The
child who never knew pity starts to know it. The child who never
belonged begins to know the delight of belonging—and begins to
respond to the love that is flowing into his heart.

A prayer

*Lord God, I marvel at the way you can transform our lives through your love. Let
your love keep on flowing into my heart and never let me put up a barrier to stop it. I
delight to say to you 'You are my God'. I want to know you more deeply and love
you more deeply every day of my life here on earth—and then through all eternity.*

New birth

There was a man sent from God... He was not that Light, but was sent to bear
witness of that Light. That was the true Light, which lighteth every man that cometh
into the world. He was in the world, and the world was made by him, and the world
knew him not. He came unto his own, and his own received him not. But as many as
received him, to them gave he power to become the sons of God, even to them that
believe on his name: which were born, not of blood, nor of the will of the flesh, nor of
the will of man, but of God.

A human child is born from its father's seed rooting and growing in its
mother's womb, nourished by her blood. But that is not how a child of
God is born. Neither is it born because human beings decide that it should
be—as a husband and wife will decide to have a child. A child of God is
born when God takes the initiative and sends his Spirit and his Word to a
human being who will receive him. The new birth of a Christian is different from the birth of Jesus—but it is something like that. 'The holy Spirit
will come upon you, and the power of the Most High will overshadow
you; therefore the child to be born will be called holy, the Son of God...'

The power that Jesus gives to us to become the sons of God is the
power of an endless life—a new life within us, which starts a new relationship of love with the God who loves us. We realize that we're loved—
though the realization might dawn very slowly. Sometimes we can hardly
dare to believe it—and our own unbelief will be like a cloud that blocks
off the light of the sun. But God created us in order to love us and for us
to return his love—so we can pray to know 'the love of God, that passes
knowledge'.

A prayer

'...God has poured out his love into our hearts by means of the Holy Spirit, who is
God's gift to us' (Romans 5:5, GNB).

Be still and pray for the gift of the Spirit and that you might really know God's love
for you.

As I have loved you

Then God said, 'Let us make man in our image, after our likeness; and let them have dominion over the fish of the sea, and over the birds of the air, and over the cattle, and over all the earth, and over every creeping thing that creeps upon the earth.' So God created man in his own image, in the image of God he created him; male and female he created them. And God blessed them . . .

The earth and its creatures have to be subdued to some extent if the human creatures are to have their proper place. But we are to subdue and have dominion as men and women made in the image and likeness of God. God has blessed us, so if we are God-like we shall bless the earth and all the creatures that live in it. That is what we are supposed to have done. What we *have* done is to use and abuse what we should have blessed, and now the earth and the creatures are dying. We are very deaf if we don't hear their voice crying out to us for help and for healing—and perhaps as Christ came to us for our healing, so we should go to the earth.

Max Warren said that when Christ looked down from the cross he didn't just see lost souls, he saw lost soil. Perhaps when we hear Christ saying to us, 'Love one another as I have loved you', we shouldn't limit that loving to human creatures. Perhaps we should love the whole earth, and all the creatures that God has made. The Good News Bible says that when the creation was finished, 'God looked at everything he had made, and he was very pleased.'

A prayer

Lord, may we love all your creation, all the earth and every grain of sand in it. May we love every leaf, every ray of your light. May we love the animals; you have given them the rudiments of thought and joy untroubled. Let us not trouble it; let us not harass them, let us not deprive them of their happiness, let us not work against your intent. For we acknowledge unto you that all is like an ocean, all is flowing and blending, and that to withhold any measure of love from anything in your universe is to withhold that same measure from you.

F. Dostoevsky

Really satisfied

Then the Lord showed concern for his land; he had mercy on his people. He answered them: 'Now I am going to give you corn and wine and olive oil, and you will be satisfied. Other nations will no longer despise you. I will remove the locust army that came from the north and will drive some of them into the desert. Their front ranks will be driven into the Dead Sea, their rear ranks into the Mediterranean. Their dead bodies will stink. I will destroy them because of all they have done to you... Animals, don't be afraid. The pastures are green; the trees bear their fruit, and there are plenty of figs and grapes.'

The Good News Bible translation that we are using says that 'the Lord showed concern for his land'—and the original word for 'showed concern' means jealous, or zealous. And in certain situations jealousy is just the right thing to feel—and it can lead to just the right action. A husband or a wife is right to be jealous if the marriage is under threat from another woman or another man. The prophet Hosea fought for his marriage, and pleaded with his wife in a mixture of anger and heartbroken love: 'I will allure her, and bring her into the wilderness, and speak tenderly to her. And there I will give her her vineyards, and make the Valley of Achor a door of hope' (Hosea 2:14–15, RSV).

When Jesus found the traders in the temple at Jerusalem defiling it with their selling of sacrificial animals, he drove them out of the temple in holy anger, and John's Gospel quotes Psalm 69:9: 'Zeal for your house will consume me' (REB).

What Hosea wanted, and what God wanted (and always wants), is to bless and to satisfy. A lover always wants to be the source of the beloved's satisfaction and happiness, and the delight is mutual. We hardly dare to believe that we can be a source of delight to God, but it says that we are. When God created the world, Wisdom was there with him 'delighting in the sons of men' (Proverbs 8:31, RSV). And the New Testament tells us that Christ is the wisdom of God, and that it was through Christ that God made the world.

Reflect

What would you like God to do for you—and for your nation? What would it be like to be really satisfied—not with food and drink but with God? We are created for union and communion with God—and it is only the love of God that can ever totally satisfy our hearts.

The man who loves sheep

I am looking out of my window on to a field filled with two dozen Jacob sheep... black and brown and white and all very woolly. The man they belong to is with them. He shepherds them in the day-time... into the section of the field where they are to eat (it has a fence down the middle, and first they eat the grass in one half and then in the other). He shepherds them at night-time... shutting them safely into their wooden shed on cold winter evenings and when they are lambing. But the man whom they belong to doesn't keep them for their wool. He keeps them because he loves them... and as I look out of my window I can watch the relationship between him and his sheep.

The word of the Lord came to (Ezekiel): 'Son of man, prophesy against the shepherds of Israel; prophesy and say to them: "This is what the Sovereign Lord says: Woe to the shepherds of Israel who only take care of themselves! Should not shepherds take care of the flock? ... You have not strengthened the weak or healed the sick or bound up the injured. You have not brought back the strays or searched for the lost ... I am against the shepherds and will hold them accountable for my flock. I will remove them from tending the flock ... I myself will tend my sheep and make them lie down, declares the Sovereign Lord. I will search for the lost and bring back the strays. I will bind up the injured and strengthen the weak, but the sleek and the strong I will destroy. I will shepherd the flock with justice."'

God is speaking to church leaders. But we are all shepherds in our own field... to our families, our friends, our workmates. We all have the task of loving and caring and feeding... giving all that is needed to grow and develop. For some of them we have to provide a safe place of shelter. The man I can see from my window does all that his sheep need. Do we?

A prayer

Lord Jesus Christ, you are the good shepherd and you gave your life for the sheep. Thank you that you did—and for all it cost you in tears and agony and pain—for me, and for the world that you love. I pray for the people who shepherd me. I pray for myself, and for the sheep that I am responsible for. Help all of us to be good shepherds.

The
HOLINESS
of
GOD

The good wine of God

My loved one had a vineyard on a fertile hillside. He dug it up and cleared it of stones and planted it with the choicest vines... Then he looked for a crop of good grapes, but it yielded only bad fruit... What more could have been done for my vineyard than I have done for it? When I looked for good grapes, why did it yield only bad? Now I will tell you what I am going to do to my vineyard: I will take away its hedge, and it will be destroyed... I will make it a wasteland, neither pruned nor cultivated, and briers and thorns will grow there... The vineyard of the Lord Almighty is the house of Israel, and the men of Judah are the garden of his delight. And he looked for justice, but saw bloodshed; for righteousness, but heard cries of distress.

God the gardener, deeply disappointed with his gardening. God the pleader, asking sorrowfully what more he could have done to make his vineyard grow. No good grapes, so no good wine. So God the gardener will make the vineyard into a wasteland, and instead of vines there will be thorn bushes.

But we know that one day there will be good wine. The people of God in that day didn't get it right. They refused to be the fruit-bearing vine they were meant to be. So the Word became flesh, and God-in-Christ was born in a stable, rather than an inn, because there was no room for him. Then he grew up—and told the world the good news in words and in actions. He said 'I am the light of the world', and the ancient people of God hadn't got that right either. They wanted to keep the light to themselves—the light that God wanted to shine in the whole world. And those people were hopeless shepherds to the flock. So God came and shepherded the flock himself: 'I am the good shepherd,' Jesus said, 'and the good shepherd gives his life for the sheep.' And just before he gave his life he took the cup, gave thanks and offered it to them, saying, 'Drink from it, all of you. This is my blood of the covenant, which is poured out for many for the forgiveness of sins' (Matthew 26:27–28).

Reflect

'I am the vine; you are the branches. If a man remains in me and I in him, he will bear much fruit; apart from me you can do nothing.' (John 15:5)

Powerful stuff...

He told them another parable. 'The kingdom of heaven is like leaven which a woman took and hid in three measures of flour, till it was all leavened.'

If you have ever made bread you will know about the amazing qualities of yeast. The tiny spores of a fungus, it can live in a dry state for years (mine lives in a blue tin in my refrigerator), but when it is given the right food and the right conditions it will start to grow. I put a tablespoon of the dried yeast into a small bowl with a teaspoonful of sugar and some warm water—and within minutes things start to happen. There is an unmistakable smell, and a pale brown, frothy mixture visibly increasing in my bowl. Then I add that to three pounds of stoneground flour and two pints of warm water and knead it. I cannot see the yeast any more—but it is still there, still working, invisible and powerful. The dough that half-filled my bread tins rises to the rim of them—then I put them into the oven and bake them for 45 minutes—and usually cut off a crust and butter it and eat it while it is still hot!

In Jesus' day they didn't have dried yeast in little blue tins. His mother would have kept back one piece of raw, leavened dough to put in the next batch of bread that she made—and the effect would start all over again. The tiny yeast, or leaven, transforms the whole of the bread that it is put into. And the kingdom of heaven is like that. It affects the whole of society. Our society's attitude to sick people and old people was transformed by the yeast of the kingdom. It was Christianity that started to look after the poor and the ill and the old. Barclay says that 'Christianity was the first faith to be interested in the broken things of life'. Christianity transformed things for women too—and if the women's liberation movement want to name their real founder they can print the name of Jesus of Nazareth on all their literature.

A prayer

Lord Jesus, I thank you for the powerful changes that the kingdom of God works in the whole of society—in broken lives and in evil places. Show me what I can do to work with you in the work of your kingdom.

The uncleanness inside us

Jesus called the people to him again, and said to them, 'Hear me, all of you, and understand: there is nothing outside a man which by going into him can defile him; but the things which come out of a man are what defile him.' And when he had entered the house, and left the people, his disciples asked him about the parable. And he said to them, 'Then are you also without understanding? Do you not see that whatever goes into a man from outside cannot defile him, since it enters, not into his heart but his stomach, and so passes on?' (Thus he declared all foods clean.) And he said, 'What comes out of a man is what defiles a man. For from within, out of the heart of man, come evil thoughts, fornication, theft, murder, adultery, coveting, wickedness, deceit, licentiousness, envy, slander, pride, foolishness. All these evil things come from within, and they defile a man.'

A woman died in our local hospital. She was a drug smuggler, and her tragic story was on the next morning's news. To get them through the customs at Gatwick she had swallowed over a hundred packets of drugs. But she never made it, because on the plane they started to disintegrate inside her body. But Jesus wasn't talking to people about drugs or poisons. He was speaking about the ritual food laws set out in the Old Testament, which said that some things were clean to eat and some were unclean. But to eat a food that was ceremonially unclean didn't make a person morally unclean, and it didn't defile a man or make a woman impure. Our real impurity comes out of our own hearts, because our hearts aren't pure.

There is a natural bent in our heart towards evil. We can call it self-centredness if we prefer, or by some other name. But no one in their wildest dreams could say that we were loving to one another all the time. So we need a heart transplant—and if we ask the Divine Physician he will give us one. A new heart, and a new spirit. Like his own. They will start small, like a baby growing in its mother's womb. But then they will grow up, and mature, and we shall become more and more like Jesus. We need food to make us grow. The milk of the word, according to Peter. And the bread and wine of Holy Communion. So feed on him in your new heart by faith, with thanksgiving.

Five vital virtues

*Finally, all of you, have unity of spirit, sympathy, love of the brethren, a tender heart
and a humble mind. Do not return evil for evil or reviling for reviling; but on the
contrary bless, for to this you have been called, that you may obtain a blessing. For
'He that would love life and see good days, let him keep his tongue from evil and his
lips from speaking guile; let him turn away from evil and do right; let him seek peace
and pursue it. For the eyes of the Lord are upon the righteous, and his ears are open to
their prayer. But the face of the Lord is against those that do evil.'*

Unity of spirit is not an optional extra but absolutely essential. Sections of
the church disagree on important issues. But we shall only glorify the
name of Christ if we love one another and affirm the truths which we do
believe in common. We are to be sympathetic, with the sin and sorrow of
the world: to weep with those who weep and rejoice with those who
rejoice, because we can feel their sorrows with them and feel their joys.
When someone is desperately sad, sometimes all we can do is to sit in
silence and somehow suffer with them. We are to love our brothers and
sisters in the faith: to want the best for them and to pray for the best. We
are to have a tender heart. Perhaps to allow ourselves to feel the suffering
of the world and to pray and take action when we see hungry, weeping
children, and hear of people dying and being hideously crippled on the
roads, because we drive so selfishly. Finally, we are to have a humble mind,
or humility, which comes from realizing that we are creatures and that
God is our Creator. We couldn't create a fly, let alone the worlds—and it
is God in Christ who holds the worlds and us in existence.

To think about

*Spend some time reflecting on the five Christian qualities of unity, sympathy, love,
compassion and humility, and consider how developed each one is in your own life.*

Our new clothes

...You must no longer live as the Gentiles live... You were taught to put away your former way of life, your old self, corrupt and deluded by its lusts, and to be renewed in the spirit of your minds, and to clothe yourselves with the new self, created according to the likeness of God in true righteousness and holiness... Do not grieve the Holy Spirit of God, with which you were marked with a seal for the day of redemption. Put away from you all bitterness and wrath and anger and wrangling and slander, together with all malice, and be kind to one another, tenderhearted, forgiving one another, as God in Christ has forgiven you. Therefore be imitators of God, as beloved children, and live in love, as Christ loved us...

I have just bought a pale-pink safari jacket—and when I wear it I feel great. It is new and pretty and people like it. My old safari jacket, which I loved, has worn out and had patches on it. I am sorry to see the end of it—but the time comes when we need to buy new clothes, and they have a different feel to them from old clothes. The Bible uses different images to describe the Christian life and the Christian's relationship to God: sometimes we are 'born again' into the family and sometimes we are 'adopted'. And we are also to 'clothe' ourselves with the 'new self'.

My new pink jacket is new and clean at the moment and I want to keep it that way. So I don't wear it while making the tomato sauce for my pasta—or even while eating the pasta, in case it gets splashed. If it does get a stain on it, though, I shall immediately sponge it clean with water. It is like that with our new self, and the stains that we make by our sinning. But when we sin we can take ourselves to the cleaners and be washed clean again in the blood of Christ. Then we can get on with living the new life, checking out our actions, and aware that sin grieves the Holy Spirit who lives within us.

A reflection

See yourself clothed in your new self—and work out how to imitate God and live in love in every area of your life.

He still eats with sinners

[Jesus] went away to the lake-side. All the crowd came to him, and he taught them there. As he went along, he saw Levi son of Alphaeus at his seat in the custom-house, and said to him, 'Follow me'; and Levi rose and followed him. When Jesus was at table in his house, many bad characters—tax-gatherers and others—were seated with him and his disciples; for there were many who followed him. Some doctors of the law who were Pharisees noticed him eating in this bad company, and said to his disciples, 'He eats with tax-gatherers and sinners!' Jesus heard it and said to them, 'It is not the healthy that need a doctor, but the sick; I did not come to invite virtuous people, but sinners.'

Jesus still eats at his table with sinners. At every service of Holy Communion we always confess our sins before we eat the bread and wine of the sacrament. The self-righteous have no place at the Lord's table. We always come as sinners—although forgiven sinners—and at the heart of our sinfulness is our failure to love. Someone hurts us or, even worse, hurts someone we love. Then we have to struggle with the pain and try to forgive and to love.

We may not have done many 'things which we ought not to have done', but we have almost certainly left undone a large number of 'those things which we ought to have done'. To take just one example, two-thirds of the world is full of hungry people—while our third of it struggles to lose weight. The problem seems so enormous that we want to turn away from it because we just don't know what we can do. But the risen Christ at whose table we eat and drink is also the source of all wisdom—and if we ask he will give us the wisdom to know what we *can* do.

'Follow me!' he said to Levi, and Levi did—one step at a time along the way, following the one who is the life and the truth and the way. So when we come to the table in the house of God we can pray first of all in deep thankfulness that he invites us to come, that he forgives our sins, and that he feeds us with himself. Then we can pray, 'Lord, what would you have me to do?'—and know that he will certainly tell us.

I will guide you . . .

So Abram went, as the Lord had told him; and Lot went with him. Abram was seventy-five years old when he departed from Haran. And Abram took Sarai his wife, and Lot his brother's son, and all their possessions which they had gathered, and the persons that they had gotten in Haran; and they set forth to go to the land of Canaan. When they had come to the land of Canaan, Abram passed through the land to the place at Shechem, to the oak of Moreh. At that time the Canaanites were in the land. Then the Lord appeared to Abram, and said, 'To your descendants I will give this land.' So he built there an altar to the Lord, who had appeared to him.

Abram did as he was told—and on his journey he came to the place in Canaan where there was a turpentine tree (a terebinth)—the famous 'oak of Moreh'. Moreh means 'oracle giver' and it was almost certainly a sacred tree. The Canaanites worshipped false gods—and took their guidance from them. A friend of mine from Africa, Jo, tells how his grandfather would throw down the bones of a chicken on to the floor of the tent when people from his village wanted guidance. It came through the way the bones arranged themselves—and Jo often saw them move after they had been thrown down. There was no doubt about it, so he found it bewildering when a sophisticated Christian minister arrived in his village and insisted it was simply imagination. Jo had seen these things happen, and he knew there was power there. He also knew that it was not the power of God.

It was God who was guiding Abram and in the face of the false gods the one, true God reiterated his promise to him: 'To your descendants I will give *this* land.' So Abram built an altar there—to the Lord of the whole earth—and worshipped the father of lights in the darkness of Canaan.

A thought

I will instruct you and teach you the way you should go; I will counsel you with my eye upon you (Psalm 32:8).

Our helper God

For I, the Lord your God, hold your right hand; it is I who say to you, 'Do not fear, I will help you.' Do not fear, you worm Jacob, you insect Israel! I will help you, says the Lord; your Redeemer is the Holy One of Israel. Now, I will make of you a threshing sledge, sharp, new, and having teeth; you shall thresh the mountains and crush them, and you shall make the hills like chaff. You shall winnow them and the wind shall carry them away, and the tempest shall scatter them. Then you shall rejoice in the Lord; in the Holy One of Israel you shall glory.

If she really knows what God is like, Israel need never be afraid. God holds her with his right hand, and as he does so the power of the living God flows into her. God loves Israel, but he knows her for what she is—faithless and powerless, unless she responds to his love and receives his strength. She is as weak as a worm, and as insignificant as an insect (and that word could be 'louse').

Yet she was still created in the image and likeness of God, and made to be indwelt by the living God and to live in relationship with him. Created to be a nation of priests and a holy nation. And if she (and if we) will allow it, the worm will be transformed into a threshing sledge. To thresh something is to separate the grain from the chaff—a picture of judgment.

Sometimes the mere presence of a holy person can make someone aware of their own sinfulness. It is as if the presence of light shines into the darkness and reveals someone's life as it really is.

A reflection

Think about your own weaknesses. Imagine that God-in-Christ, who is Jesus, is holding your hand with his right hand. Believe that he can help you—and thank him that he will. Then remember the words of Jesus: 'I am the light of the world' (John 8:12). 'You are the light of the world... let your light shine before others, so that they may see your good works and give glory to your Father in heaven' (Matthew 5:14–16).

The message of God

This is the message we have heard from him and proclaim to you, that God is light and in him there is no darkness at all. If we say that we have fellowship with him while we are walking in darkness, we lie and do not do what is true; but if we walk in the light as he himself is in the light, we have fellowship with one another, and the blood of Jesus his Son cleanses us from all unrighteousness.

I have just had two burglar lights installed, and on the first night they were fitted the friends who were having dinner with me said, 'Stop talking! Look!' And there in the light was a most beautiful fox—probably looking for some more of the kidneys which I had cleared out from my freezer the day before.

The light shows us what is there. A fox or a burglar in my security lights. Good or evil in the light of God, whose nature and being is light. The nature of light is to shine, and it is the nature of God to reveal himself. He did it perfectly in Jesus. 'The true light that gives light to every man was coming into the world' says John in his Gospel (1:9), and it happened when the Word became flesh—the Word who was with God in the beginning, and the Word who was a person alive with the life and the light of God: 'In him was life, and that life was the light of men…' (John 1:4). The light of the love of God (because the being of God is also love) shows us ourselves as we really are. Sinners. But all the time greatly loved—and all the time having the guilt of our sins washed away through the blood of Christ. As we walk in the light we shall know the love of God for us, and also the beautiful moral perfection and purity of the God whose name is Holy. Then we shall change, and be more and more like him.

To reflect on

We who… contemplate the Lord's glory, are being transformed into his likeness with ever-increasing glory, which comes from the Lord, who is the Spirit… For God, who said, 'Let light shine out of darkness,' made his light shine in our hearts to give us the light of the knowledge of the glory of God in the face of Christ.
(2 Corinthians 3:18; 4:6)

Matter matters

In the beginning was the Word, and the Word was with God, and the Word was God.
The same was in the beginning with God. All things were made by him, and without
him was not any thing made that was made.

One of the reasons why John was so insistent that all things were made by the Word, who was God, is that there was a heresy around which said that matter was evil.

The heresy was Gnosticism, and Gnostics had worked out a theory that two things existed in the beginning: God *and* matter. They did it to try to explain the evil in the world, and they said that the matter was evil and that the world was made out of it. God was pure spirit, and couldn't have anything to do with this evil stuff—and the world was made by a series of emanations from God which got further and further away from him until the final emanation was 'so distant from God that it was totally ignorant of God and totally hostile to God—and this emanation was the power which created the world... To the Gnostics the creator God was a God who was utterly divorced from and utterly at enmity with the real God' (Barclay).

In Colossians 1:16 Paul wrote, 'For by him all things were created: things in heaven and on earth... all things were created by him and for him.'

C.S. Lewis wrote, 'God likes matter—He invented it'—and it makes a very important difference to our lives if we believe that. Everything that is matters, and everything is holy—because everything was made (and is still being made and held in existence) by a holy God.

A meditation

Touch something close at hand—and feel its texture and its solidness. Think of the
Creator God speaking the word of creation right back at the beginning... the word
that was God himself, and is God... and consider that whatever you are touching and
feeling is made from the matter that God has made. Look at your hands, and touch
them—and be aware that God has made the matter of which you are made. God isn't
a long way off, beyond the stars—although he is there too. He is with you, closer than
breathing. He holds the stars and you in existence—and he loves you.

The promise of God

*Now when they heard this, they were cut to the heart and said to Peter and to the
other apostles, 'Brothers, what should we do?' Peter said to them, 'Repent, and be
baptized every one of you in the name of Jesus Christ so that your sins may be
forgiven; and you will receive the gift of the Holy Spirit. For the promise is for you,
for your children, and for all who are far away, everyone whom the Lord our God
calls to him.' And he testified with many other arguments and exhorted them, saying,
'Save yourselves from this corrupt generation.' So those who welcomed his message
were baptized, and that day about three thousand persons were added.*

Today's passage is a marvellous summary of how to begin the Christian
life, and how to go on with it and to live it. We start by repenting—by
admitting our sins and by turning our back on them—or at least being
willing to; sometimes our sins seem to draw us as powerfully as drugs
draw an addict. The power of God, however, is greater than the power of
sin, and there is a promise of a powerful helper—God the Holy Spirit—to
live in us. But first comes forgiveness, and then baptism, to signify the
washing away of sin and the drowning and death of the old life. Perhaps
it isn't pushing symbolism too far to think of the water as a new womb for
a new birth.

Then comes the gift of the Holy Spirit, which is the gift of God—and
the promise running right down the years to us and to our children. We
are living in a corrupt generation just as those early disciples were, and
equally need to be saved and delivered from it. Three thousand were
saved and delivered on the Day of Pentecost—and then they started to live
out the new life within them. The Bible says how they sustained it. 'They
devoted themselves to the apostles' teaching and to the fellowship, to the
breaking of bread and to prayer...' Four things for the Christian to do
which are like the four legs of a table—if one goes missing or is shorter
than the others, then the table either falls over or has to be propped up.
So ask yourself, Is the table of your Christian life steady?

The royal law

If you really keep the royal law found in Scripture, 'Love your neighbour as yourself,' you are doing right. But if you show favouritism, you sin and are convicted by the law as law-breakers. For whoever keeps the whole law and yet stumbles at just one point is guilty of breaking all of it. For he who said, 'Do not commit adultery,' also said, 'Do not murder.' If you do not commit adultery but do commit murder, you have become a law-breaker. Speak and act as those who are going to be judged by the law that gives freedom, because judgment without mercy will be shown to anyone who has not been merciful. Mercy triumphs over judgment!

Every Christian is a member of a royal priesthood—and this priesthood has a law. The royal law of love, James calls it. The Old Testament had told us to love our neighbour as ourselves, and so does the New. But the New Testament makes it quite clear who our neighbour is. The astonishing story of the Good Samaritan (it would have astonished its first hearers when Jesus told it because Samaritans were looked down on and priests and scribes were looked up to) shows us who Jesus sees as our neighbour, and shows us how people who keep this law actually treat their neighbours. It isn't loving to love a rich man and look down on a poor man. That is to break the royal law of love—and to break even one section of the law is to be a guilty person. That is true with human laws as well as God's laws—if we should ever be prosecuted for a parking offence, it won't help our case one jot to tell the magistrate that we haven't broken any of the laws relating to theft or murder or mugging. To break even one law is to have earned and to deserve the penalty that goes with it—and the New Testament and the Old both say that 'the wages of sin is death'. What we earn and deserve through any sin is spiritual death, because all sins separate us from God.

A thought

Do I keep the royal priesthood's royal law of love?

The ruin of the city

Come down and sit in the dust, virgin daughter Babylon! …hear this, you lover of pleasures… You felt secure in your wickedness; you said, 'No one sees me.' Your wisdom and your knowledge led you astray, and you said in your heart, 'I am, and there is no one besides me.' But evil shall come upon you, which you cannot charm away; disaster shall fall upon you, which you will not be able to ward off; and ruin shall come on you suddenly, of which you know nothing. Stand fast in your enchantments and your many sorceries, with which you have laboured from your youth; perhaps you may be able to succeed, perhaps you may inspire terror. You are wearied with your many consultations; let those who study the heavens stand up and save you, those who gaze at the stars, and at each new moon predict what shall befall you.

Babylon was a great city—and she stands for all the cities of the world who live for pleasure and who preen themselves in their own glory instead of delighting in the glory of God. Babylon is the city that is not the city of God. But godlessness contains in itself a seed of self-destruction—and the city that is not of God will eventually suffer ruin and disaster. It seems to be happening all around us in the western world. On the whole, we are godless. Some of us talk about being 'a Christian nation'—but those are empty words and not a living reality. Politicians and the media called for Christian values to be taught again in our schools and to our young people—because two young children of ten were convicted of murdering a little boy of just two years old, who put his hand in theirs and walked trustfully away with them out of a huge shopping complex in a large city. But Christian values cannot stand without Christians—and as Christians we can only stand in the power of our God. Some in the City of London consult the stars to see what they should do with their finances and their business deals. But that consultation won't help them. The only one who can help is the one who created the stars.

A prayer

Almighty and most merciful Father, creator of all things, judge of all men, have mercy on the godless cities of our world—and help us who know you to shine with your light in the dark places of the earth.

The everlasting light

There came a man who was sent from God; his name was John. He came as a witness to testify concerning that light, so that through him all men might believe. He himself was not the light; he came only as a witness to the light.

The darkness of sin has made a barrier between the human race and God—and the only way for people to know God was for him to destroy the barrier and reveal himself. The Old Testament tells us a great deal about the nature of God and the glory of God. For the Jew the Word of God was a lamp for his path and a light on his way—and Isaiah wrote of a day when people would no longer need the sun or the moon to see by, 'for the Lord will be your everlasting light, and your God will be your glory. Your sun will never set again, and your moon will wane no more; the Lord will be your everlasting light, and your days of sorrow will end' (Isaiah 60:19–20).

The Jews knew that God was the light—but the nation as a whole was failing to let it shine out all over the world. So through Isaiah God says of his servant, 'It is too small a thing for you to be my servant to restore the tribes of Jacob and bring back those of Israel I have kept. I will also make you a light for the Gentiles, that you may bring my salvation to the ends of the earth' (Isaiah 49:6).

The task of John the Baptist was to testify to the Light. To tell people who the Light was—so that through that knowledge all people (not just the Jews) could believe. The light had been shining in the hearts of every human being ever since God had created the human race. Some of them knew the God who was the source of their light. But now the Light himself was coming into the world in human form.

Reflect

Think about how you experience the Light in your own life. If someone asked you to tell them about it, what would you say and how would you witness to it?

A solemn warning

One year, in London's famous Regent Street, the Christmas decorations were angels blowing trumpets. Shoppers went to and fro down below, gazing up at the illuminated angels and admiring them. But some of us gave rather wry smiles. In biblical visions angels do not blow their trumpets for joy. They blow them for judgment.

Then I saw the seven angels who stand before God, and seven trumpets were given to them... The first angel blew his trumpet, and there followed hail and fire, mixed with blood, which fell on the earth; and a third of the earth was burnt up, and a third of the trees were burnt up, and all green grass was burnt up. The second angel blew his trumpet, and something like a great mountain, burning with fire, was thrown into the sea; and a third of the sea became blood, a third of the living creatures in the sea died, and a third of the ships were destroyed.

As the other angels blow their trumpets other disasters happen on the earth. In three plagues a third of mankind is killed. But...

The rest of mankind, who were not killed by these plagues, did not repent of the works of their hands... nor did they repent of their murders or their sorceries or their immorality or their thefts.

We live in a world where these things are happening all around us. Thousands of murders and muggings a year... rape... witchcraft and astrology. Ordinary burglaries and 'higher-class' theft in the shape of frauds in the city and false income-tax declarations. Trees being burnt up with acid rain. The cleansing power of the sea being destroyed by pollution, as we pour untreated effluent into it, and spill great oil slicks through our wicked carelessness, so that the seals and the fish and the seabirds die. The trumpets of judgment are blowing, and perhaps we are starting to repent. If we do, things will change.

A prayer

Lord God, you created our world and you told us to have dominion over it. Help us to repent of our abuse of it. Help us to love it and to heal it. Help us—and help me—to keep your commandments... 'Thou shalt not kill'... 'Thou shalt not commit adultery'... 'Thou shalt not steal'...

Tell them the good news!

Otherwise, what will those people do who receive baptism on behalf of the dead? If the dead are not raised at all, why are people baptized on their behalf? And why are we putting ourselves in danger every hour? I die every day! That is as certain, brothers and sisters, as my boasting of you—a boast that I make in Christ Jesus our Lord. If with merely human hopes I fought with wild animals at Ephesus, what would I have gained by it? If the dead are not raised, 'Let us eat and drink, for tomorrow we die.' Do not be deceived: 'Bad company ruins good morals.' Come to a sober and right mind, and sin no more; for some people have no knowledge of God. I say this to your shame.

Today some friends are coming to lunch. We have just arranged it on the telephone, and I am planning the meal in one bit of my brain while I write these notes with the rest of it. Pasta with a sauce of sun-dried tomatoes, garlic and Greek yoghurt, with a green salad and a Bulgarian red wine. I love cooking, and eating and drinking—and so do they. But if all the good things of this life come to an end when we die then we had better make the most of them—even though there is a sadness at the heart of them.

But Paul knew that there is another life after this one, and because it mattered so much to him that other people should know it too—and share it—after his encounter with the risen Christ on the road to Damascus he spent the rest of his life telling the world the wonder of the good news. But he couldn't do it all himself, and the Corinthians (and presumably we too) should be ashamed that some people still have no knowledge of God.

A prayer

Lord Jesus Christ, thank you that this life isn't the end of the story when we know you. Help us to tell the greatest love story in the world to the people who don't know it, so that they might know God.

Right or rite?

Your New Moon festivals and your appointed feasts my soul hates. They have become a burden to me; I am weary of bearing them. When you spread out your hands in prayer, I will hide my eyes from you; even if you offer many prayers, I will not listen. Your hands are full of blood; wash and make yourselves clean. Take your evil deeds out of my sight! Stop doing wrong, learn to do right! Seek justice, encourage the oppressed. Defend the cause of the fatherless, plead the case of the widow. 'Come now, let us reason together,' says the Lord. 'Though your sins are like scarlet, they shall be as white as snow; though they are red as crimson, they shall be like wool.'

Someone I know is very religious. He loves all the rites and rituals that go on in his church, and he is meticulous about getting them correct. But he is very wary of a relationship with God, and deeply dislikes prayers that are personal and tender and full of praise. Sometimes I wonder if his religion isn't a way for him to protect himself from God rather than a way through to God. God alone knows if I am right—and strictly the matter is one for God and that man to work out between them. Whether I am right or wrong, I can pray, and however feeble my praying is, God will gather it up into his purposes and use it as a means of doing his will in the world.

The prophet Isaiah was very clear that the religious rites of Judah and Jerusalem were offensive to God and he simply wasn't interested in what they were doing. He wanted them to do right. To 'stop doing wrong and to learn to do right!' The poor were oppressed. Orphans and widows weren't being looked after. If they would do what they were supposed to do then (and only then) would their scarlet sins be as white as the driven snow—a promise that is often torn out of its context and attached to the moment when a person commits his or her life to Christ. Jesus calls us to follow him—and that means to follow his example and imitate his life.

A prayer

Lord Jesus Christ, you were the friend of outcasts and sinners. You fed the hungry. I want to follow you and to imitate you. Show me if I am using my religion and my churchgoing to hold you at arm's length. If I am, draw close to me, and help me to stop it.

In tune with God

For those who live according to the flesh set their minds on the things of the flesh, but those who live according to the Spirit set their minds on the things of the Spirit. To set the mind on the flesh is death, but to set the mind on the Spirit is life and peace. For this reason the mind that is set on the flesh is hostile to God; it does not submit to God's law—indeed it cannot, and those who are in the flesh cannot please God.

A person who lives 'in the flesh' cannot possibly live in tune with God, because the word 'flesh' actually means to live out of tune with God, and to have a will that is out of line with the will of God. We cannot sing out of tune and in tune at the same time. And to be 'in the flesh' is to sing out of tune.

But in the Spirit we do sing in tune with the will of God. We are in Christ, and the Spirit of Christ is in us, and now we can submit to God's law and do the will of God. We don't always, even once our new life has begun, but we *can*. Faith is the secret of it. In chapter 1 Paul writes, 'I am not ashamed of the gospel: it is the power of God for salvation to everyone who has faith, to the Jew first and also to the Greek. For in it the righteousness of God is revealed through faith for faith; as it is written, "He who through faith is righteous shall live"' (Romans 1:16, 17). To be righteous is to be in a right relationship with God, with all our sins forgiven (and being forgiven every day) and with the Holy Spirit within us to help us to live a holy life of love. The last verse of Charles Wesley's marvellous hymn 'And Can It Be' sums it all up.

Reflect

No condemnation now I dread;
Jesus, and all in Him, is mine!
Alive in Him, my living Head,
And clothed in righteousness divine,
Bold I approach the eternal throne,
And claim the crown, through Christ my own.

Shine and be salty

'You are the salt of the earth; but if salt has lost its taste, how can its saltiness be restored? It is no longer good for anything, but is thrown out and trampled under foot. You are the light of the world. A city built on a hill cannot be hid. No one after lighting a lamp puts it under the bushel basket, but on the lampstand, and it gives light to all in the house. In the same way, let your light shine before others, so that they may see your good works and give glory to your Father in heaven.'

In the summer my mother would sit in the garden with a big bowl of salt on one side of her and a heap of runner beans on the other. My father had grown them on his allotment, and she was slicing them up and layering them with salt for us to eat in the winter. The salt stopped the beans decaying—and the task of the Christian Church is to stop the decay and corruption of the world we live in. But salt can lose its saltiness. Then there is corruption—and the putrid, horrible smell of evil, violence and injustice.

The Church is also the light of the world. But our light can grow dim, and in the western world I think it has. Then the darkness gets deeper. If a local or a national church refuses to repent then the Christ who is the light of the world will come to us and take away the candlestick that holds the light—and that church will be only a name in the pages of history. But we can repent and turn back to the Christ who is the head of the Church, and respond to the words that he spoke to the church of Laodicea, which was 'wretched, pitiful, poor, blind and naked', and wasn't aware of it: 'Here I am! I stand at the door and knock. If anyone hears my voice and opens the door, I will come in and eat with him, and he with me' (Revelation 3:20).

Next time you go to Communion, will you think about the Church as the salt of the earth and the light of the world. Then, as you receive bread and wine, receive the one who knocks at the door and longs to come in and revive the Church which is his body and his bride.

Success that never ends

Thus says the Lord, your Redeemer, the Holy One of Israel: I am the Lord your God, who teaches you for your own good, who leads you in the way you should go. O that you had paid attention to my commandments! Then your prosperity would have been like a river, and your success like the waves of the sea; your offspring would have been like the sand, and your descendants like its grains; their name would never be cut off or destroyed from before me.

Some years ago the Institute of Advanced Legal Studies in the University of London moved into a new building—and the Institute bought some new furniture, including two expensive desk chairs purchased from a high-class shop. They had only been in use a few days when one of them collapsed as the librarian sat on it. Two weeks later, the ex-principal of the university sat in the other, and that collapsed as well. 'But they were such *good* chairs,' wailed the woman who had bought them. But 'good' is just what they were not, because they lacked the essential quality of supporting people who sat in them—obviously the function of a 'good' chair!

When God teaches us or the Israelites, we need to realize that goodness in the Old Testament 'means the desire to create such things as fellowship, trust, joy and wholeness in the minds of others' (Knight). This is what God wants to create in his people, and if we let him do it for us then we can do genuine good to others, showing real love and compassion.

If Israel had only listened, and let the life-giving and creative words of God enter into her, then her spiritual life would have been like a river and her effectiveness would have been like the waves of the sea—one wave following another in an unbroken succession. Then, as they saw the presence and the Holy One of Israel living and working within his people, other people would have joined the family of the faithful—so many that they couldn't be counted, any more than the grains of sand on the seashore can be counted. That was the promise that God gave to Abraham, the father of the faithful.

A way to pray

Imagine yourself on the seashore. Reflect on the infinite number of grains of sand—and on the waves breaking in foam at your feet, one after the other without ending. Ask God to teach you 'for your own good', so that you might be effective for him in the world that he loves. Remember how much he loves you and yearns after you.

The champagne of God

Be sure of this, that no fornicator or impure person, or one who is greedy (that is, an idolater), has any inheritance in the kingdom of Christ and of God. Let no one deceive you with empty words, for because of these things the wrath of God comes on those who are disobedient. Therefore do not be associated with them. For once you were darkness, but now in the Lord you are light. Live as children of light—for the fruit of the light is found in all that is good and right and true... Do not get drunk with wine, for that is debauchery; but be filled with the Spirit...

Perhaps the reason why the Bible isn't very popular reading these days is that people don't like what it says. Even Christians fornicate and commit adultery. Anything can be forgiven as long as we 'know' it needs to be forgiven. These days, though, we hardly regard sexual sins as sins at all. However, God doesn't want us to stop sinning in order to spoil our fun, but to make us really happy. After all, he invented sex—we didn't!

Chastity is tough, especially for anyone who has experienced a sexual relationship (or relationships). However, it is possible, and the deprivation of it can drive us to God to find a satisfaction that is beyond all believing. Jesus called us to take up our cross daily and follow him, and this can be one of the ways to do it. We need the death and denial of our false self—and a flooding in of a new life that bubbles like champagne. We are not drunk with wine, though, but instead we are filled with the Spirit.

A way to pray

In silence, allow the Holy Spirit to show you your life as he sees it, in every area. Ask him to help you to repent, if you need to. Then ask him to fill you with his Spirit, and remember that on the day of Pentecost they thought that Peter and the rest of the disciples were drunk.

The light of life

Again Jesus spoke to them, saying, 'I am the light of the world; he who follows me will not walk in darkness, but will have the light of life.'

The Jews didn't know all the things about light that our generation knows. They didn't know that it was an energy of undulating particles, and that the colour of the light varied according to the length of the wave. But they knew some things about light—and perhaps they were more important things. They knew that it shone into the darkness at the foundation of the world. They knew that God spoke his word in the darkness—'Let there be light' (Genesis 1:3).

They knew that light showed them the way in the darkness. For them the word of God was like light—'Thy word is a lamp to my feet, and a light to my path' (Psalm 119:105). They also knew that the name of God was 'I am...' And now a man is standing in the midst of them and saying, 'I am the light of the world' and promising that if they followed him they wouldn't walk in the darkness but would have the light of life.

Jesus would have known the great passages in Isaiah about the suffering servant of God, and it was in line with the Old Testament promises and prophecies that he said he was the light of the world. 'It is too light a thing that you should be my servant to raise up the tribes of Jacob and to restore the preserved of Israel; I will give you as a light to the nations, that my salvation may reach to the end of the earth' (Isaiah 49:6).

Jesus is the light of the world—and so are we. He says so in the Sermon on the Mount, and tells us to shine. 'You are the light of the world. A city set on a hill cannot be hid. Nor do men light a lamp and put it under a bushel, but on a stand, and it gives light to all in the house. Let your light so shine before men, that they may see your good works and give glory to your Father who is in heaven' (Matthew 5:14–16).

A prayer

Jesus, light of the world, shine on me. Shine into my heart like the brightness of the sun. Shine into the dark places of my life with your pure shining, and shine into the darkness of the world—especially those parts of it that I now hold in your shining presence...

Root out evil

The word of the Lord came to me: 'And you, O son of man, thus says the Lord God to the land of Israel: An end! The end has come upon the four corners of the land. Now the end is upon you, and I will let loose my anger upon you... and I will punish you for all your abominations. And my eye will not spare, nor will I have pity; but I will punish you according to your ways, while your abominations are in your midst. Then you will know that I am the Lord, who smite.'

This year a small plant with vicious purple and yellow flowers took root in the dark corner where my dustbin lives. Then the flowers turned into bright green, round berries, which ripened to scarlet. Deadly nightshade. I intended to root it out before, but there were other more interesting things to do. Today, when I tried to dig it up, I found a cancerous network of white roots running underground. Unlike my blackberry bush, which is ripening now into sweet, good, luscious fruit, the deadly nightshade has poisonous fruit. 'Injustice has blossomed, pride has budded. Violence has grown up into a rod of wickedness; none of them shall remain, nor their abundance, nor their wealth' (vv. 10–11). God will let these things grow and blossom and bear a crop of poisonous fruit—and if we don't root them out then he will let loose his anger and do it himself. If we allow evil to flourish in our land and in our lives, the crop we grow will be the food we eat. Don't let us fool ourselves that God doesn't get angry. What would a normal parent feel towards the drugs baron who got rich on the 'crack' that was destroying her child?

A meditation

Think of some of the things happening in our land and in our world... millions starving and homeless... children being sexually abused and physically ill-treated... dogs half-starved and beaten. Can a holy, loving God not mind? What fruit are we eating from our injustice and our social cruelty? Is it the violence and fear in our streets? How can we root out the evil?

Where is the fruit?

In the morning, as he was returning to the city, he was hungry. And seeing a fig tree
by the wayside he went to it, but found nothing on it but leaves only. And he said to
it, 'May no fruit ever come from you again!' And the fig tree withered at once. When
the disciples saw it they marvelled, saying, 'How did the fig tree wither at once?' And
Jesus answered them, 'Truly, I say to you, if you have faith and never doubt, you will
nto only do what has been done to the fig tree, but even if you say to this mountain,
'Be taken up and cast into the sea,' it will be done. And whatever you ask in prayer,
you will receive, if you have faith.'

There are two incidents in Jesus' life which do not fit in with many people's
view of him. One is the time when he turned over the money-changers'
tables in the temple and drove them out with a whip of small cords. The
other is the one in our reading today. But when Jesus does something
unusual it is sensible to pay special attention to it.

This acted parable is about fruitfulness and barrenness. In Mark's
account of the same story it has the phrase 'it was not the season for figs',
but if we brood too much about that we shall miss the parable's main
point. God created the fig tree, and his people, to bear fruit. 'By their fruits
you shall know them,' Jesus said in one place, and also, 'By this is my
Father glorified, that you bear much fruit.' A fig tree covered in beautiful
shining green leaves, with no fruit, is barren.

Christianity isn't about outward show. It is about a relationship with
the living God that results in good works. 'Bear fruit that befits repentance,' Jesus told his hearers on another occasion. This story of what Jesus
did to the fig tree shakes us to our roots and we find ourselves horrified.
But one day we shall stand before the Christ who is going to be the judge
of our lives, and the test of our faith will be the fruit of our lives.

Meditation

Imagine yourself as a fig tree… and imagine Jesus coming to you to pick your fruit.
What do you think it will be? Then imagine your local church as a fig tree… Will he
find fruit on you that satisfies him?

All lost for Christ

...I myself have reason for confidence in the flesh also. If any other man thinks he has reason for confidence in the flesh, I have more: circumcised on the eighth day, of the people of Israel, of the tribe of Benjamin, a Hebrew born of Hebrews; as to the law a Pharisee, as to zeal a persecutor of the church, as to righteousness under the law blameless. But whatever gain I had, I counted as loss for the sake of Christ.

Paul had been everything a Jew could ever want to be. If getting it right as a Jew was what could give a man real confidence in God then Paul had it all. He had been circumcised on the proper day—the eighth day. He was an Israelite who could trace his descent from Jacob—to whom God had given the new name of Israel after his all-night wrestling match at Jabbok. He was of the tribe of Benjamin, which was the highest of all the tribes of Israel—the aristocracy. He was born of a Hebrew mother and a Hebrew father—which meant that they (and he) actually spoke Hebrew. So his blood and his language were the best—utterly pure. He was a Pharisee—trained in the Jewish law.

Paul had kept the law, which would have meant all the endless rituals and regulations of the Jewish law—far heavier than the biblical regulations of the Old Testament (though in Romans he says that the Old Testament law finally showed him that he was a sinner: 'I should not have known what it is to covet if the law had not said, "You shall not covet"...' Romans 7:7). Paul knew it all—and in terms of his status as a Jew he'd got it all. But in terms of getting himself into a right relationship with God all those things were useless. They weren't a gain. They were a loss. All because of the encounter which Paul (Saul, he was, then) had with the risen Christ on the road to Damascus, when the whole of his life was turned around, and he worshipped the one whom he had persecuted.

A question

In your relationship with God, in what—or in whom—do you put your confidence? Think what it must have been like for Paul, the proud Pharisee, to abandon all his Jewish credits for the sake of Christ.

Friends with our enemies

So then, remember that at one time you Gentiles... were... aliens from the commonwealth of Israel, and strangers to the covenants of promise, having no hope and without God in the world. But now in Christ Jesus you who once were far off have been brought near by the blood of Christ. For he is our peace; in his flesh he has made both groups into one and has broken down the dividing wall, that is, the hostility between us. He has abolished the law with its commandments and ordinances, that he might create in himself one new humanity in place of the two, thus making peace, and might reconcile both groups to God in one body through the cross, thus putting to death that hostility through it.

In the temple at Jerusalem a Jew went through various courtyards to get to the inner court, where the Holy of Holies stood at the centre, veiled from everyone by a thick curtain. Only the high priest could enter the holiest place, and that only once a year. Women could come in as far as the court of the women, and Gentiles as far as the court of the Gentiles. But between the court of the Gentiles and the rest of the temple there was a wall, with tablets set into it warning that if a Gentile went any further he was liable to be put to death. But now Paul is saying that that wall has been broken down—and so have all the walls, though he doesn't say so here. In the Gospels it says that at the very moment when Christ died the great curtain which separated the people from God in the Holy of Holies was torn from the top to the bottom—and the way into the presence was open.

Now all the walls are down, and people who were once enemies can be reconciled and know the peace of God. Now 'there is no longer Jew or Greek, there is no longer slave or free, there is no longer male or female; for all of you are one in Christ Jesus' (Galatians 3:27–28). Paul wasn't saying that a Jew was no longer a Jew, or that slavery would instantly be abolished, or that women and men were the same. He was writing of the barriers to friendship and real love between all those groups. But it all has to be worked out in our daily living and we still aren't managing it very well.

A way to pray

Pray for peace in Christ in the battle of the sexes and between ethnic groups who despise each other in our nation and in our world.

A shining priesthood

Depart, depart, go out thence, touch no unclean thing; go out from the midst of her, purify yourselves, you who bear the vessels of the Lord. For you shall not go out in haste, and you shall not go in flight, for the Lord will go before you, and the God of Israel will be your rear guard.

God is calling his people to come out of captivity and to come home. The Jews were physically exiled from their own, God-given land. They were slaves in Babylon, where the inhabitants worshipped false gods. But the people of God are to be the slaves and the servants of God and obey only him. In a sense we live in exile all the time, in a world that neither knows God nor worships him. Instead it worships the gods of money, success and comfort. But we can still be at home in God even in the midst of 'a crooked and depraved generation, among whom (we) shine like stars in the universe as (we) hold out the word of life' (Philippians 2:15).

Those 'who bear the vessels of the Lord' were those from the priestly tribe, and they were to purify themselves. But all the people of Israel had been called to be priests—and in the book of Exodus God told Moses of his plan and his purpose, and promised to guide them and to carry them. 'You have seen what I did to the Egyptians, and how I bore you on eagle's wings and brought you to myself. Now, therefore, if you will obey my voice and keep my covenant, you shall be my own possession among all peoples, for all the earth is mine, and you shall be to me a kingdom of priests and a holy nation' (Exodus 19:4–6).

In the New Testament Peter picks up all those beautiful promises to the Jewish people and applies them to Christians.

A prayer

Lord God, help me—and all the members of your Church—to purify ourselves, and to be the royal priesthood you have called us to be, so that we may bring men and woman to you and you to men and women. Amen.

By his life . . .

Therefore, since we are justified by faith, we have peace with God through our Lord Jesus Christ ... While we were still weak, at the right time Christ died for the ungodly. Why, one will hardly die for a righteous man—though perhaps for a good man one will dare even to die. But God shows his love for us in that while were yet sinners Christ died for us. Since, therefore, we are now justified by his blood, much more shall we be saved by him from the wrath of God. For if while we were enemies we were reconciled to God by the death of his Son, much more, now that we are reconciled, shall we be saved by his life.

When we are given the cup at Holy Communion, we drink, and the person who gives it says to us, 'The blood of Christ keep you in eternal life' (or some similar phrase). We are using the Old Testament symbols of sacrifice—blood poured out sacrificially in death, because 'the life of the flesh is in the blood'. Just as it costs us to forgive another person—because we bear the pain of the injury, and go on loving—so it costs God. When John the Baptist saw Christ coming towards him he said, 'Behold, the lamb of God, who takes away the sin of the world.'

In *The Lion, the Witch and the Wardrobe* Aslan tells the children that 'though the Witch knew the Deep Magic, there is a magic deeper still which she did not know ... If she could have looked... into the stillness and the darkness before Time dawned, she would have read there a different incantation. She would have known that when a willing victim who had committed no treachery was killed in a traitor's stead, the Table would crack and Death itself would start working backwards...'

Strong stuff, for Aslan to talk of traitors and the apostle Paul to talk of enemies. But we can have an almost implacable resistance to the love of God and the demand it makes on us, and we don't want to admit that failure to love God and our neighbour which is theologically called 'sin'. But once we have said 'yes' to all of that, we know a peace that we never knew before, and the risen life of the Christ who died becomes our life and gives health to our souls...

Love minds so much

And I shall feel no pity for her children since they are the children of her whorings.
Yes, their mother has played the whore, she who conceived them has disgraced herself by
saying, 'I shall chase after my lovers; they will assure me of my keep, my wool, my
flax, my oil and my drinks.' This is why I shall block her way with thorns, and wall
her in to stop her in her tracks; then if she chases her lovers she will not catch them, if
she looks for them she will not find them, and then she will say, 'I shall go back to my
first husband, I was better off then than I am now'; she had never realized before that
I was the one who was giving her the grain, new wine and oil…'

Do you wonder how a God of love can possibly speak in this way through
a prophet? Do you think that God and Hosea ought to go on pitying us
whatever we do, and that our Maker ought not to mind? But how can love
not mind? If the person you love most in the world came and told you that
she or he had murdered a man, raped a woman, sexually abused a child,
or robbed a bank, would you really not mind? You would go on loving
them—but the more you loved them, the more you would mind.

So God minds most of all. God gives us everything—our life, our earth,
our food and our drink. So it must provoke him if we give the credit to
other sources. How would we feel if we gave someone a beautiful present
and they thanked someone else for it? Multiply that by a million and we
start to see what God has given us. But he doesn't give up. The things that
we have been enjoying seem to slip through our fingers—perhaps when
God withdraws his pity (his sympathetic sorrow for one suffering) and
allows us to suffer the consequences of our actions. Then our suffering
and lack of pleasures drive us back to him.

A prayer

God of love, I find it surprising that you still want someone who comes back to you
just because they are hungry and have nowhere else to go. But then I remember the
prodigal son and the waiting father. I am glad you are like that—and I am glad that
you mind so much when we sin, because you love us so much.

The
MAJESTY
of
GOD

Creative words

In the beginning God created the heavens and the earth. The earth was without form and void, and darkness was upon the face of the deep; and the Spirit of God was moving over the face of the waters. And God said, 'Let there be light';
and there was light.

In *The Magician's Nephew* by C.S. Lewis, there is a marvellous account of how Aslan creates Narnia:

'The Lion was pacing to and fro about that empty land and singing his new song. It was softer and more lilting than the song by which he had called up the stars and the sun; a gentle, rippling music. And as he walked and sang the valley grew green with grass. It spread out from the Lion like a pool. It ran up the sides of the little hill like a wave. In a few minutes it was creeping up the lower slopes of the distant mountains, making that young world every moment softer...'

The only way we can ever talk about anything is to use words. But the words are only descriptions of reality—and what the Bible writers (and modern physicists) are doing when they speak about the creation of the world is struggling to describe a mystery in words that we can understand.

'God said, "Let there be light."' A creative energy went forth from God and everything began. Many scientists now believe in the 'big bang' theory —that at a moment at the beginning of time (because before that moment there was no time) something mysterious and mighty exploded into existence, from which everything that is developed.

God spoke his creative word in the darkness, and the heavens (the galaxies spinning round in space) came into existence—and then, perhaps after thousands of millions of years of creation, men and women like you and me, being created by the God of love to have a relationship with him for ever.

A meditation

Think of C.S. Lewis's Lion pacing round and singing the song that brings the grass into existence. Then think of the unfathomable mystery of the Creator God speaking the word that brought all things into existence... including you and me.

Spirit and truth

*'I see you are a prophet, sir,' said the woman. 'Our fathers worshipped on this
mountain, while you say that Jerusalem is the place where one ought to worship.'
Jesus said: 'Believe me, woman, the hour is coming when you will worship the Father
neither on this mountain nor in Jerusalem. You worship what you do not know; we
worship what we do know: for salvation comes from the Jews. But the hour will
come—in fact it is here already—when true worshippers will worship the Father in
spirit and truth: that is the kind of worshipper the Father wants. God is spirit, and
those who worship must worship in spirit and truth.' The woman said to him, 'I
know that Messiah—that is, Christ—is coming; and when he comes he will tell us
everything'. 'I who am speaking to you,' said Jesus, 'I am he.'*

Today I looked at a friend's face as he struggled to put into words the con-
flicts and emotions in his mind. But no one except him knows all the
thoughts in his mind. 'For what person knows a man's thoughts except
the spirit of the man which is in him?' (1 Corinthians 2:11, RSV). No ordinary human being knows—but there is someone who does. Someone who
is both human and divine: the Son of God whose Spirit is in us if we
belong to him. He totally understands us—and he knows us far better
than we know ourselves.

'Now I know in part; then I shall understand fully, even as I have been
fully understood' wrote St Paul in 1 Corinthians 13:12 (RSV) or (NRSV)
'then I will know fully, even as I have been fully known.' He was writing
about the future glory of heaven, where we shall be worshipping God
without ceasing. Then the sons and daughters of the living God (which we
are now, if we are Christians) will live with their heavenly Father for ever
and ever, delighting in being the bride of Christ.

But although in the glory of heaven we shall worship God perfectly,
with total delight and with the whole of our being, we can worship and
praise him now. We praise the glory of God in Christ—because we are in
the Spirit and the Spirit of Christ is in us. And we praise and worship
because of the truth we know—through the whole of the Christian story,
told in the Bible and by the Church. So we worship 'in spirit and in truth'.
That is what God wants us to do.

Now answer me!

Then the Lord answered Job out of the tempest: 'Who is this who darkens counsel
with words devoid of knowledge? Brace yourself and stand up like a man; I shall
put questions to you, and you must answer. Where were you when I laid the earth's
foundations? Tell me, if you know and understand... On what do its supporting
pillars rest? Who set its corner-stone in place, while the morning stars sang in chorus
and the sons of God all shouted for joy? ... Can you bind the cluster of the Pleiades
or loose Orion's belt? Can you bring out the signs of the zodiac in their season or
guide Aldebaran and its satellite stars? Did you proclaim the rules that govern the
heavens or determine the laws of nature on earth?'

We might think that God could have talked to Job about his suffering—
instead of taking him on a guided tour of the universe and its extraordinary creatures. But Job has been longing for God to talk to him ever since
his sufferings began. Now the Creator is doing just that—through his creation. Job has been speaking his mind. Now God is going to speak his.

If we sometimes feel a bit envious of other people who seem to know
God better than we do, then it might be that they are better at listening to
the voice of God than we are. One of the ways to hear his voice is to reflect
on the creation. Not the whole of it—which we couldn't do anyway—but
just a part of it. Look at a tree... or at a single leaf. Really look at it. Look
at the sky, and the colours of it... dark grey and pale grey, and blue and
pink and red. Watch the clouds scudding by... and the birds flying. Or read
the Bible reflectively, and slowly, and ask God to speak to you as you read.
But wait...and listen. Start writing a spiritual journal. Not every day. But
write what you are thinking and feeling, and put down your questions.
Then wait, expectantly. You will know the voice—but what it says may
surprise you.

A way to pray

Are there any questions that you want to fling at God—or simply to ask him
quietly—about what is happening either to you, to someone else, or to the world?
If there are, ask them. Be blunt, and be honest. Then listen for the voice of God.
But remember that you may have to wait for it.

Praise the Lord

Praise the Lord.
Praise God in his sanctuary;
praise him in his mighty heavens.
Praise him for his acts of power;
praise him for his surpassing greatness.
Praise him with the sounding of the trumpet,
praise him with the harp and lyre,
praise him with tambourine and dancing,
praise him with the strings and flute,
praise him with the clash of cymbals,
praise him with resounding cymbals.
Let everything that has breath praise the Lord.
Praise the Lord.

If we want to know where to praise God, the answer is everywhere. God is in his sanctuary—and God is everywhere. 'Where can I go to escape your presence?' asks the writer of Psalm 139 and the answer to that is 'Nowhere!' Because wherever we go God is there. That isn't a reason for dread (except for the right sort of holy awe), but for delight. We praise him on earth—and we join our praise 'with the whole company of heaven'. Our reason for praising him is that he is God—and that he is a God of love. He is the creator of the whole earth and he made all things. You and me, the seas and all the creatures who live in them, the sky and all the living things that fly in it, and the earth and all its plants and creatures—as well as all the stars in the galaxies of the Milky Way.

God the creator is also God the redeemer—so with all the means we have at our disposal we praise him. Sometimes noisily, sometimes quietly. In every way we want, and in every way we choose. And not just human creatures: 'Let everything that has breath praise the Lord.' The blackbird that runs round on my lawn, praises the Lord simply by being a blackbird; sometimes singing its heart out; sometimes sunning itself on the earth with its wings spread out and its beak wide open. Perhaps our task as a royal priesthood is to gather up all creatures and all things and praise God through our delighting in them. But I think they existed to the praise of the glory of God during all the time before man and woman existed on earth, and this psalm says that in the glory of heaven they will be praising God together with us and the angels.

The holy Presence

In the year that King Uzziah died, I saw the Lord sitting on a throne, high and lofty; and the hem of his robe filled the temple. Seraphs were in attendance above him, each with six wings: with two they covered their faces, and with two they covered their feet, and with two they flew. And one called to another and said: 'Holy, holy, holy is the Lord of hosts; the whole earth is full of his glory.' The pivots on the threshold shook at the voices of those who called, and the house was filled with smoke. And I said, 'Woe is me! I am lost, for I am a man of unclean lips, and I live among a people of unclean lips; yet my eyes have seen the King, the Lord of hosts!'

Uzziah had been king of Israel for the whole of Isaiah's life. Now he had died. But there was another king who was king of the whole earth and whose glory filled the whole of the earth. Isaiah saw his glory in a vision in the earthly temple, surrounded by seraphs. Seraph means 'burning one', but even these bright creatures cover their faces with their wings in the presence of the Lord of glory. Utter holiness and transcendent purity devastate Isaiah—and he sees himself as he is. He was called to speak the word of God, but his own lips were unclean. So were the lips of the whole people of God, who were called to be 'a nation of priests', and to praise God. But how can words of praise to a holy God be spoken through unclean lips? The solution to that problem lies with God, because the holy and transcendent God is also immanent, which means 'indwelling, inherent; actually present or abiding in; remaining within' (*Shorter Oxford Dictionary*). He has revealed himself to Isaiah in the temple—and he reveals himself to us. The holiness and the presence together will deal with our problem—and then we can sing out his praises and tell the world about his glory and his power to save.

A way to pray

Reflect on Isaiah's vision and on the holiness of God—and pray that he will show you yourself in the bright light of his glory.

Daily thanksgiving

It is good to give thanks to the Lord, to sing praises to thy name, O Most High; to declare thy steadfast love in the morning, and thy faithfulness by night, to the music of the lute and the harp, to the melody of the lyre. For thou, O Lord, hast made me glad by thy work; at the works of thy hands I sing for joy. How great are thy works, O Lord! Thy thoughts are very deep! The dull man cannot know, the stupid cannot understand this . . .

Yes, I did. I gave thanks to the Lord soon after I awoke this morning. I can't say I sang praises, and certainly there was no accompaniment of lute and harp. One of my deficiencies—I have many—is that I can't play any musical instrument—but I went over in my mind causes for thanksgiving. I try to do this at the beginning of each day. There is always something for which to praise God, though apparently quite small, trivial. And at night before I go to sleep I run over in my mind the good things that have happened, frequently most ordinary things, like the garden machinery mechanic who said he would call to collect my mower for servicing and he did! Our psalm today says, 'It is good to give thanks to the Lord, to sing praises to thy name, O Most High.' And then this: 'the dull man cannot know, the stupid cannot understand this'. We are far more likely to be well in body and mind if we give proper place to thanksgiving in our lives. Discontent and ingratitude pull us down.

A few weeks ago I nearly 'came a cropper' on this resolve to keep the good and lovely things in mind; I thought I would let the garden go a bit this year. And then my eye caught a little cluster of snowdrops blooming merrily outside my study window and I was rebuked. They were praising God in their way. And it will not be long after Easter before that blackbird starts filling the garden with his song as he does every spring (is it the same one?) even though he will find some of the branches in the silver birch tree lopped off where he usually perches. So I will make a point of making my garden as decorative as I can. God has given us good and lovely things and we praise God, the Creator, by caring for them and rejoicing in them, and are better people for doing so.

Prayer

Lord, I praise you for the good things you have given me—my garden, lovely flowers, the kindness of neighbours and the love of some particular people, but above all for the wonder of Easter with its message of newness of life.

Abiding word

You have been born anew, not of perishable seed but of imperishable,
through the living and abiding word of God; for

'All flesh is like grass
and all its glory like the flower of grass.
The grass withers, and the flower falls,
but the word of the Lord abides for ever.'

That word is the good news which was preached to you.

The 'word' that God speaks—the word of good news—will never die like
the grass. Therefore neither will we—because we are born of a seed that
is eternal seed.

A human baby is born when a woman's tiny egg is fertilized by a man's
even tinier seed—and then grows within her womb, nourished and protected, until it's ready to be born. The mother will labour, and then a baby
girl or a baby boy will come into the world and utter its first cry. But one
day, whether as a child or an adult, that baby will die. Its flesh is perishable—like goods on supermarket shelves marked with a 'sell-by' date.
Soon after that date, the milk will go sour and the chicken will go off…
They don't keep for ever—and neither do we. We might die at seven
months, seven years, or seventy years or more. But die we shall.

We're like grass that withers and dies—and like daisies and dandelions:
beautiful for a few days but then the flowers fall. They aren't everlasting—
and even so-called everlasting flowers are really dead and dried flowers.

But there can be that in us which is everlasting. We can be born of an
imperishable seed, 'the living and abiding word of God'.

A way to pray

Think of fresh food on the shelves of a supermarket—eatable, but perishable. Think
of daisies and dandelions growing in a park—beautiful, but perishable. Think of
yourself, and all the people that you love—just as perishable as food and flowers. But
then think of Jesus Christ, who is the word of God—alive, and (if we believe)
dwelling in our hearts by faith.

'I am the resurrection and the life; he who believes in me, though he die, yet shall
he live, and whoever lives and believes in me shall never die' (John 11:25–26).

Pray with Paul . . .

For this reason I bow my knees before the Father, from whom every family in heaven and on earth takes its name. I pray that, according to the riches of his glory, he may grant that you may be strengthened in your inner being with power through his Spirit, and that Christ may dwell in your hearts through faith, as you are being rooted and grounded in love. I pray that you may have the power to comprehend, with all the saints, what is the breadth and length and height and depth, and to know the love of Christ that surpasses knowledge, so that you may be filled with all the fulness of God. Now to him who by the power at work within us is able to accomplish abundantly far more than all we can ask or imagine, to him be glory in the church and in Christ Jesus to all generations, forever and ever. Amen.

Paul has written about the wonder of the plan of salvation, and about the purpose of God for his Church. Having set it out in its glory, he now prays that the Church will live it out. Then the glory will shine out. We can pray Paul's prayer for ourselves as individuals and for the Church as a whole. Pray it for the people in our local church—and for the leaders of the Church throughout the world. Think again of the astonishing power that is available to us: the power of God who created the world and who raised Christ from the dead. It is ours for the asking—if we meet the conditions. And the conditions are that we ask and pray, and that we are a holy people. We are anyway, in one sense, because we are the people of God and we belong to God. That makes us holy. But holy people need to live holy lives, and we manifestly don't. God, though, can change us. He can change me and he can change you. He can change the Church. And he can change the world.

A way to pray

Pray Paul's prayer for yourself, and for your church.

The heavenly marriage

Then I saw a new heaven and a new earth; for the first heaven and the first earth had passed away, and the sea was no more. And I saw the holy city, new Jerusalem, coming down out of heaven from God, prepared as a bride adorned for her husband; and I heard a loud voice from the throne saying, 'Behold, the dwelling of God is with men. He will dwell with them, and they shall be his people, and God himself will be with them; he will wipe away every tear from their eyes, and death shall be no more, neither shall there be mourning nor crying nor pain any more, for the former things have passed away.' And he who sat upon the throne said, 'Behold, I make all things new.'

There is a glorious and beautiful tangle of mixed metaphors in the Bible. God is the good shepherd—and the good shepherd gives his life for the sheep. Jesus is both the shepherd and the Lamb of God who takes away the sin of the world. God is the husband of his people—and now a holy city is coming down out of heaven like a bride adorned for her wedding and the wedding will be the marriage supper of the Lamb.

Heaven is union and communion with God-in-Christ—a union far more intimate than any human marriage. But the human marriage can tell us things about the heavenly one. The prophet Hosea loves and marries an unfaithful and adulterous bride and then buys her back from slavery and goes on loving her. In the Song of Songs there is an enormous and mutual delight of the Lover and the Beloved, the bridegroom and the bride, and Jews and Christians have always seen in this a picture of the love relationship that there is between God and his people. When we are in love what we most want is to be in the presence of the beloved—and to make love is to express physically what we feel in our whole being. The biblical metaphors about the wonder and the glory of heaven point to a blissful union that is beyond any human union and a consummation beyond believing.

A way to pray

Reflect on human marriage, and let it show you something of the relationship between Christ and his Church.

Refining fire

You have wearied the Lord with your talk. You ask, 'How have we wearied him?'
By saying that all evildoers are good in the eyes of the Lord, that he is pleased with
them, or by asking, 'Where is the God of justice?' I am about to send my messenger to
clear a path before me. Suddenly the Lord whom you seek will come to his temple; the
messenger of the covenant in whom you delight is here, here already, says the Lord
of Hosts. Who can endure the day of his coming? Who can stand firm when he
appears? He is like a refiner's fire, like a fuller's soap; he will take his seat, testing
and purifying; he will purify the Levites and refine them like gold and silver, and so
they will be fit to bring offerings to the Lord.

'Where is the God of justice?' they have asked—and Malachi says that they
are about to find out, because he is about to come to his temple in judgment. But with God one day is as a thousand years and a thousand years
as one day, and the people who asked the question will have died by the
time this prophecy has its fulfilment.

Matthew, Mark and Luke all quote the first half of 3:1: 'I am about to
send my messenger to clear a path before me,' and they all make the verse
refer to John the Baptist. Mark then quotes a verse from Isaiah: 'Prepare
the way of the Lord, make his path straight.' It is the Lord of Hosts who
will come, say the prophets. And he does—named Jesus, because he will
save his people from their sins.

It is frightening to think of being put in a refiner's fire, so that the
impurities in us rise to the surface and can be removed. But it isn't an
impersonal fire. It is the presence of Christ himself. John sees him in the
revelation he is given on the Isle of Patmos: '...his eyes flamed like fire, his
feet were like burnished bronze refined in a furnace, and his voice was like
the sound of a mighty torrent. In his hand he held seven stars, and from
his mouth came a sharp two-edged sword; his face shone like the sun in
full strength. When I saw him, I fell at his feet as though I were dead'
(Revelation 1:14–17).

A reflection

See in your mind's eye a picture of the risen Christ as John describes him. Stay in his
presence. Know that he loves you. Then ask him to speak to you and purify you.

The light of the world

God in his mercy has given us this work to do, and so we are not discouraged. We put aside all secret and shameful deeds; we do not act with deceit, nor do we falsify the word of God. In the full light of truth we live in God's sight and try to commend ourselves to everyone's good conscience. For if the gospel we preach is hidden, it is hidden only from those who are being lost. They do not believe, because their minds have been kept in the dark by the evil god of this world. He keeps them from seeing the light shining on them, the light that comes from the Good News about the glory of Christ, who is the exact likeness of God. For it is not ourselves that we preach; we preach Jesus Christ as Lord, and ourselves as your servants for Jesus' sake. The God who said, 'Out of darkness the light shall shine!' is the same God who made his light shine in our hearts, to bring us to the knowledge of God's glory shining in the face of Christ.

A way for us to reflect on this passage is to apply it to our own life—and to be drawn into worship as we contemplate the wonder and the nature of the Good News. We may not all be preachers in the strict sense, but each one of us is a light in the world. So pray that the Spirit will bring into the light anything that you have hidden in the darkness—so that your light will shine more brightly. Think about the people you know from whom the gospel seems to be hidden. Pray for them—that they will start to hate the darkness they are living in, and long for the light. Pray that they will see the glory of the light of Christ, who is the exact likeness of God—'a friend of sinners', and 'a man of sorrows'. Reflect on the glory of God— shining in the face of Christ, and praise God for the day when he called you out of darkness into his marvellous light (even if you don't know what day it was) and made you a new creature and a new creation—just as millions of years ago he commanded the light to shine in the darkness and created the worlds.

The way to God

Then will the eyes of the blind be opened and the ears of the deaf unstopped. Then will the lame leap like a deer, and the mute tongue shout for joy. Water will gush forth in the wilderness and streams in the desert. The burning sand will become a pool, the thirsty ground bubbling springs... And a highway will be there; it will be called the Way of Holiness. The unclean will not journey on it; it will be for those who walk in that Way; wicked fools will not go about on it... But only the redeemed will walk there, and the ransomed of the Lord will return. They will enter Zion with singing; everlasting joy will crown their heads. Gladness and joy will overtake them, and sorrow and sighing will flee away.

Recently I heard of a Christian woman who had been totally blind ever since she was born. The person telling me the story had asked her: 'Do you resent it that you have been blind all your life?' 'No', she said, 'because the first thing that I shall ever see will be Jesus—when I see him in heaven!'

The highway Isaiah writes about is the ancient caravan highway that pilgrims travelled along on their way to Jerusalem. But the earthly road is a symbol of the spiritual way to God, and Zion stands for the spiritual centre of the whole earth. The whole of creation is going to share in the glory and the redemption of the people of God. But it hasn't happened yet—for the creation or for us. We are only half way to heaven—but we are on the Way, the Way of Holiness. We follow Jesus—who said 'I am the way, the truth and the life.' In the book of Isaiah there are many references to 'the Holy One of Israel', and in the Gospels, Jesus is called 'the Holy One of God'.

A way to pray

Look back to the Old Testament prophecies... Look back to the birth of the Holy One of God two thousand years ago in a place where there was no room for him. Now, as we look ahead to our own redemption, can we look to our own holiness. Pray that we may reflect the glory of God and the light of Christ, and bring the living water of God into a dark and thirsty world.

I Am Almighty

When Abram was ninety-nine years old the Lord appeared to Abram, and said to him, 'I am God Almighty; walk before me, and be blameless. And I will make my covenant between me and you, and will multiply you exceedingly.' Then Abram fell on his face; and God said to him, 'Behold, my covenant is with you, and you shall be the father of a multitude of nations. No longer shall your name be Abram, but your name shall be Abraham.'

God is revealing his nature to Abram by telling him his name—El Shaddai, which means God Almighty. This name is used in passages which stress the power of God in contrast to human helplessness (Job calls on El Shaddai thirty-one times during his sufferings). 'It was the claim of El Shaddai to be powerful where man was weakest, and He exerts this claim supremely by promising to an obscure and numerically tiny family that they should one day possess and populate a land which, in their day, was inhabited and owned by people immeasurably their superiors in number and power' (J.A. Motyer, in a fascinating monograph, *The Revelation of the Divine Name*, Tyndale Press 1959). God tells Abram his own name—and then he gives Abram a new name, which is also to give him a new nature. Abram means 'father exalted', but Abraham means 'father of many', and the promise is that Abraham will be the father of a multitude of nations. This is a reminder of the night when God said to him 'Look toward heaven and number the stars, if you are able to number them.' Then he said to him, 'So shall your descendants be' (15:5). The God who is almighty is the God of Abraham and all his descendants—and since Abraham is the father of all who have faith in God, that means you and me.

A meditation

Think of a situation in your life where you are deeply conscious of your weakness… and then spend two or three minutes holding it in the presence of El Shaddai… Almighty God.

The beloved creation

The wolf shall live with the lamb, the leopard shall lie down with the kid, the calf and the lion and the fatling together; and a little child shall lead them. The cow and the bear shall graze, their young shall lie down together; and the lion shall eat straw like the ox. The nursing child shall play over the hole of the asp, and the weaned child shall put its hand on the adder's den. They will not hurt or destroy on all my holy mountain; for the earth will be full of the knowledge of the Lord as the waters cover the sea.

God the Creator has made a world full of creatures—birds and fishes, insects and mammals, as well as the unique human creatures into whom he breathed his own Spirit. And in the story of creation in Genesis it says after each stage of creation that 'God saw that it was good'. The Good News Bible translates that as 'God was pleased with what he saw', and has an Annie Vallotton drawing of fish swimming in the water, a stork-like bird flapping joyfully in the air, and the sun and some stars and a small moon shining down over the creatures and over a tree, some ferns and a flower. I don't know how Annie Vallotton manages to make the creatures look so happy. Her ability flows from her skill as an artist. It's a skill that we need to learn for our environment. We have tragically failed to love it—and a symbol of our failure, burnt into my mind, is one small, oil-bedraggled sea bird struggling out of the sea polluted by yet another tanker disaster. But when (and if) we do the will of God, and allow the Prince of Peace to reign over us and over our world, then there will be a new harmony in the whole of creation. It won't happen perfectly in this life, but Paul writes of the glory that there will be on the other side of the grave.

Reflect

I consider that our present sufferings are not worth comparing with the glory that will be revealed in us. The creation waits in eager expectation for the sons of God to be revealed... the creation itself will be liberated from its bondage to decay and brought into the glorious freedom of the children of God (Romans 8:18–21).

Creation tells

The heavens are telling the glory of God;
and the firmament proclaims his handiwork.
Day to day pours forth speech,
and night to night declares knowledge.
There is no speech, nor are there words;
their voice is not heard;
yet their voice goes out through all the earth,
and their words to the end of the world.

This psalm says that the universe itself is the way that God speaks to us. We don't hear any speech or any words—yet by its very existence it has a voice that we can hear.

In Romans 1:19–20 Paul says that the world itself reveals to people that there is a God, and shows us something of what he is like. Paul is writing about wicked men who have been suppressing the truth which in their heart of hearts they know: 'For what can be known about God is plain to them, because God has shown it to them. Ever since the creation of the world his invisible nature, namely, his eternal power and deity, has been clearly perceived in the things that have been made. So they are without excuse...'

Perhaps we find it hard to believe in God, now that we know something of the vastness of the universe. But the sheer size of it need not make any difference. Scientists tell us that our human bodies are midway between the immense largeness of the starry heavens and the immeasurable smallness of the particles that our bodies and all matter are composed of. I find that fact curiously comforting, when I occasionally get afflicted with what Teilhard de Chardin called 'the malady of space-time'. It can also make me stunned and awed at the glory of God—as modern science spells out to me the amazing, wonderful speech of the stars and the universe.

A meditation

Sit in silence for a few moments and let the heavens speak to you of the glory of God.
Think of the vastness of the astronomical distances of space, and the sheer size of it all.
It may stun you and frighten you—but let it also comfort you, that our God can
make such a universe.

The glory speaks

Once, when I was reading John Macquarrie's *Principles of Christian Theology*, I had an experience which totally surprised me. Academic books of theology are not where I expect to meet God. I read Macquarrie's comments on the revelation of the divine name—'I am what I am' ... and I was suddenly so strongly aware of the presence and the glory of the living God that I had to cover my head with my duvet and hide. Somehow the glory came streaming through the words... and I was aware of the One 'who is and who was and who is to come' (Revelation 1:8).

As I write I have stopped for nearly half an hour... struggling to find words to describe the feelings of awe and dread and delight, plus the sense of knowing that this was what I was made for—to be in this relationship with this holy God. Wholly 'Other', in one sense, because pure Spirit—but whom we can know and who alone satisfies and quenches that divine longing and thirst within us.

Most of us only have little glimpses of the glory. Ezekiel had a stunning vision of it, and flat on his face before it he hears the voice of God.

He said to me, 'Son of man, stand up on your feet and I will speak to you.' As he spoke, the Spirit came into me and raised me to my feet, and I heard him speaking to me. He said: 'Son of man, I am sending you to the Israelites, to a rebellious nation that has rebelled against me; they and their fathers have been in revolt against me to this very day. The people to whom I am sending you are obstinate and stubborn. Say to them, "This is what the Sovereign Lord says." And whether they listen or fail to listen—for they are a rebellious house—they will know that a prophet has been among them. And you, son of man, do not be afraid of them or their words...'

A prayer

Lord God, the Israelites stand for all nations... all of us have rebelled against you. Help me not to rebel. Help my nation not to rebel. Show us your glory and speak to us. And may we listen to you... so that we might become a righteous nation, caring and compassionate and just, and holy.

Exactly like God

The Son is the radiance of God's glory and the exact representation of his being,
sustaining all things by his powerful word. After he had provided purification for sins,
he sat down at the right hand of the Majesty in heaven.

As I look out of my window across the fields I can see a row of poplar trees with the sun shining on them. There is a hill behind them, but they are so tall that the tops of trees are against the pale blue of the winter sky. The leaves fell off last month. But the glory of the poplar trees is in their unique shape just as much as their rustling leaves—so that the sort of tree they are, and their essential nature, still shines out of them.

The glory that shone out of Jesus was the unique nature of God. When we look at Jesus we can see what God is like. We can see what Bishop John Robinson called so beautifully 'the human face of God'. When we look with the eyes of faith we see the Son of God, who sustains everything that is by his word of power; the divine energy that goes forth and holds in being the whole of the created universe, the universe that began when God spoke his word in the darkness and said, 'Let there be light!'

The writer of this letter says that the Son is the exact representation of the being of God—like a seal stamped on wax. And the writer would know how Jesus lived his life on this earth—as the friend of publicans and sinners and as the servant who washed the feet of his disciples. And as the one who forgave men and women their sins, and who died so that their sins could be forgiven.

'After he had provided purification for sins, he sat down...' This verse says in short what other chapters will say at length: that there is no need for any more sacrifices for sin. Jesus' work of sin-bearing is completed. As he said on the cross just before he died, 'It is finished!' So now he is sitting down.

A way to pray

Read this verse from Hebrews out loud and then be silent for two or three minutes,
being aware of the presence of God, and asking that the Spirit would reveal the glory
of God to you...

The power of God in us

God put this power to work in Christ when he raised him from the dead and seated him at his right hand in the heavenly places, far above all rule and authority and power and dominion, and above every name that is named, not only in this age but also in the age to come. And he has put all things under his feet and has made him the head over all things for the church, which is his body, the fulness of him who fills all in all.

If we want power for living and for doing the will of God, then we can have it. An astonishing power, almost beyond believing. It is the power of God that raised Christ from the dead, and it is there for us. But we have to make the connection and let it in—except that the power is personal: not an 'it', but a 'he', the Holy Spirit of the living God. Sometimes our trouble is that we don't want that power.

It isn't necessarily comfortable to have the living God living in us, the God who made the world and all the stars in the milky way, and who made a new creation by raising the dead. Jesus Christ 'was crucified, dead and buried, and the third day he rose again from the dead, and sits on the right hand of God the Father Almighty'. The right hand is the place of the power of God—and through Jesus all the power of God can flow to us and through us like a river.

A river of life to give life to a poisoned and dead world. And we are the body of that Christ, so we can know the fulness of Christ, the presence of Christ, and the power of Christ for all our living and loving. If only we want it and pray for it. If only we would!

A way to pray

Will you pray for that power and that presence, for you and for the whole Church, and for your local church in particular? The world we live in is dying in the darkness—and doesn't even know that it needs the life and the love of Christ. So pray. For power, for love, and for an outpouring of the Spirit of God on the Church in our day—so that the blessing will spill over and bless the world.

The life of the world

In him was life, and that life was the light of men. The light shines in the darkness, but the darkness has not understood it.

All living things are alive because God the Son gives them life and holds them in existence. 'In the past God spoke to our forefathers through the prophets... but in these last days he has spoken to us by his Son... through whom he made the universe. The Son is the radiance of God's glory and the exact representation of his being, sustaining all things by his powerful word' (Hebrews 1:1–3).

But human creatures have a higher life than other creatures. The story of the origin of all things and all creatures says that 'the Lord God formed the man from the dust of the ground and breathed into his nostrils the breath of life, and the man became a living being'. Derek Kidner writes, '"Formed" expresses the relation of craftsman to material, with implications of both skill and a sovereignty which man forgets at his peril; while "breathed" is warmly personal, with the face-to-face intimacy of a kiss and the significance that this was an act of giving as well as making; and self-giving at that' (*Genesis*, Tyndale Press).

The life in us shines with the light of God—and we are the only creature in our world who is able to discover the structure and reflect on the meaning of that world. We can also go on a journey of self-discovery, and find that we are an astonishing mixture of good and evil, light and darkness. The image of God in us is flawed. The glory is still there—but there is a dark and a destructive side to us coexisting with the light. The light of God who created us shines in the heart of every human creature—and the darkness can never overcome it. But it can't understand or comprehend it either—and neither can the human creature until men and women get to know their Creator as their Saviour and their Father.

A way to pray

Reflect on the light and the darkness in our world. The light of learning, knowledge, kindness, healing, friendship and love. Reflect on the darkness of ignorance, cruelty, injustice and war. Ask the light of God to shine in your own heart into any dark places to love you and heal you. Then pray in the same way for some dark place in our world.

Word of light

For... we preach... not ourselves, but Jesus Christ as Lord, with ourselves as your servants for Jesus's sake. For it is the God who said, 'Let light shine out of darkness' who has shone in our hearts to give the light of the knowledge of the glory of God in the face of Christ.

Today we think about the Word which God speaks into our darkness, to bring the new creation into existence. Just as God said, 'Let light shine out of darkness' at the creation of the world, so he shines into the darkness of human hearts.

The Bible says that Christians are 'a new creation', who have seen the light of the knowledge of the glory of God (which is his nature and character) shining out of the face of Christ. That shining is a creative word from God, and more often than not we hear it through the preaching of the word, which is the gospel or the good news.

Paul says what that good news is, and what the Christian message is—that 'Jesus is Lord'. That is a tremendous claim to make—and the people who made it, right back at the beginning of Christianity, were Jews. They knew that there was only one God, Jehovah, and that he alone was to be worshipped. Yet the word 'Lord' in the New Testament is the same word that the Old Testament uses for God.

The beginning of Mark's Gospel says that John the Baptist called people to 'prepare the way of the Lord', and those words come from Isaiah, whose next sentence is 'make straight in the desert a highway for our God (Isaiah 40:3). So Mark is saying that if they will prepare the way then their God will come to them. And he does. Yet the one who comes is a man—'Jesus Christ, the Son of God' (Mark 1:1).

A prayer

Lord God, I have seen something of the light of the knowledge of your glory in the face of Jesus Christ. Let me see it shining more brightly day by day. May I walk in the light of it all the days of my life—until the dawning of that perfect day when I see him face to face and am like him.

Seeing the glory

The desert and the parched land will be glad; the wilderness will rejoice and blossom.
Like the crocus, it will burst into bloom; it will rejoice greatly and shout for joy. The
glory of Lebanon will be given to it, the splendour of Carmel and Sharon; they will
see the glory of the Lord, the splendour of our God. Strengthen the feeble hands, steady
the knees that give way; say to those with fearful hearts, 'Be strong, do not fear; your
God will come, he will come with vengeance; with divine retribution he will come to
save you.'

Isaiah 35 is about the joy and the glory of a redeemed creation—and about
the restoration of the relationship between God and his human creatures
and the whole of nature. At the start of chapter 34 Isaiah's prophetic call
was to the whole of the earth, not just to the Hebrew people: 'Come near,
you nations, and listen; pay attention, you peoples! Let the earth hear, and
all that is in it, the world, and all that comes out of it! The Lord is angry
with all nations…' Then comes a judgment that is total and universal—but
spelt out in terms of the particular judgment on Edom.

But after the universal judgment there is universal restoration. Dry and
thirsty deserts will 'blossom as the rose'—and I don't suppose it matters
much whether the word means rose or crocus. In my garden I love both
of them (though the roses flourish and the birds and the mice eat the
crocuses). I believe that in the glory of heaven they will all be there. All
flowers, all trees, and all creatures. But not all human creatures. Only the
redeemed. Only those who have been forgiven by the God of love—and
who love him in response to his love.

There is a shining glory ahead of us. So in the suffering that is going on
now we can be strong—and encourage one another. In this present darkness we can hope—and we can pray.

A way to reflect and pray

Think about the picture Isaiah paints of what lies ahead. Think about the glory of
God… the nature and the character of God made manifest, so that we can know it
and see it… the beatific vision. Think about 'the glory of God in the face of Jesus
Christ'. Reflect on the words of Jesus: 'He who has seen me has seen the Father…'
Pray to be made strong… remembering what God said to Paul, that 'my strength is
made perfect in weakness'. Then hope—and pray.

Stairway from heaven

So he became as much superior to the angels as the name he has inherited is superior to theirs. For to which of the angels did God ever say, 'You are my Son; today I have become your Father'? Or again, 'I will be his Father and he will be my Son'? And again, when God brings his firstborn into the world, he says, 'Let all God's angels worshp him.' In speaking of the angels he says, 'He makes his angels winds, his servants flames of fire.' But about the Son he says, 'Your throne, O God, will last for ever and ever, and righteousness will be the sceptre of your kingdom. You have loved righteousness and hated wickedness; therefore God, your God, has set you above your companions by anointing you with the oil of joy.'

The Jews were great believers in angels. They were the messengers of God to the human race, but they were mysterious—spiritual beings whom God had created. Sometimes they appeared as men, and only afterwards did people realize that they were angels—as in the strange story of Lot and the men of Sodom and Gomorrah (Genesis 19). Some of us in our world find it hard to believe in angels—but some say that they have both seen them and been protected by them.

In Jacob's dream he saw a stairway that came down from heaven to earth, with angels going up and down upon it, and the Lord God standing above it and speaking to him. Hundreds of years later the man Jesus is speaking to another Israelite, Nathaniel, who has doubts about who he is. But doubt turns to faith: 'Rabbi, you are the Son of God, you are the King of Israel.' Jesus replies, 'You believe because I told you I saw you under the fig tree. You shall see greater things than that... I tell you the truth, you shall see heaven open, and the angels ascending and descending on the Son of Man' (John 1:49–51).

Meditate

Contemplate Jesus Christ, Son of God and Son of Man. Then... be silent and let that truth sink into your heart.

Waiting

I consider that the sufferings of this present time are not worth comparing with the glory that is to be revealed to us. For the creation waits with eager longing for the revealing of the sons of God; for the creation was subjected to futility, not of its own will but by the will of him who subjected it in hope; because the creation itself will be set free from its bondage to decay and obtain the glorious liberty of the children of God.

Most of us find it hard to wait for things. We wait impatiently for buses and wonder why they are so late. Then (in London) three Number 11 buses turn up in a convoy and we feel impatient with the bus company. We wait for a friend to arrive—or for a special letter to come through our letter-box. We wait for the end of term and the start of the holidays.

There is a lot in the Bible about waiting—and it is always about waiting with confident hope, because what we are waiting for is something that God is going to bring about. That makes our present sufferings far more endurable. In 2 Corinthians 4:17–18, St Paul says that those sufferings are effecting something good in us: 'this slight momentary affliction is preparing for us an eternal weight of glory beyond all comparison, because we look not to the things that are seen but to the things that are unseen; for the things that are seen are transient, but the things that are unseen are eternal'.

It isn't only we who wait. It is as if the whole of the creation is waiting and longing for things to be what one day they will be. The word translated 'eager longing' describes the attitude of someone 'who scans the horizon with head thrust forward eagerly searching the distance for the first signs of the dawn break of glory. To Paul, life was not a weary, defeated waiting; life was a throbbing, vivid expectation' (William Barclay, *The Letter to the Romans*). One day all created things will be caught up in Christ. There will be a glory beyond imagining, and everything will be set free from decay.

A world of glory

Through him all things were made; without him nothing was made that has been made.

I remember particularly enjoying hearing Professor Frank Close giving the Royal Institution's Christmas lectures. 'The Cosmic Onion' was the title of them—and as I watched and listened I found myself marvelling at the wonder of the way the world is. Sometimes the intensity of my feeling— and the understanding in my mind—came together in a delighted worship of the God who created all things. I was filled with awe—and so are some scientists.

John Polkinghorne, President of Queens' College, Cambridge, and the only priest in the Church of England who is also a Fellow of the Royal Society, wrote of 'that absolutely characteristic scientific experience—an experience of wonder and marvel at the very beautiful way the laws of physics work and the balances and structures within them.' In the Christmas lectures Professor Close spoke of galaxies which are flying out into space faster than the speed of light (which is why the night sky is dark and not ablaze with light).

Polkinghorne says, 'The world is doing two things at the same time. It is flying apart and expanding because the initial, fiery singularity of the big bang blew it apart, but also gravity is at work pulling it together. If the force of expansion were too strong then the world would fly apart too quickly. It would be too dilute, and nothing would happen. But if con- traction were too strong then the world would collapse... So you need this very delicate balance between the two, and the accuracy of getting it right has been calculated as equivalent to the accuracy of hitting a target an inch wide at the other side of the universe—which is quite a crack shot!' (*Lent for Busy People*, ed. Shelagh Brown, BRF).

John is saying that all the things that the scientists know about and tell us about were made 'through him'—the Word who was there with God in the beginning. John didn't know what the scientists know. But he knew that there were stars in the sky, and that they could make us ask questions about our smallness and value in the scheme of things.

A way to pray

Reflect on John 1:3, and on these words from Psalm 8:3–4: 'When I consider your heavens, the work of your fingers, the moon and the stars, which you have set in place, what is man that you are mindful of him, the son of man that you care for him?'

The glory of God

Have this mind among yourselves, which is yours in Christ Jesus, who, though he
was in the form of God, did not count equality with God a thing to be grasped, but
emptied himself, taking the form of a servant, being born in the likeness of men. And
being found in human form he humbled himself and became obedient unto death, even
death on a cross. Therefore God has highly exalted him and bestowed on him the name
which is above every name, that at the name of Jesus every knee should bow, in heaven
and on earth and under the earth, and every tongue confess that Jesus Christ is Lord,
to the glory of God the Father.

Today's passage is a hymn of praise to the wonder and glory of Christ—
one of the greatest that has ever been written. If, as Christians, we want to
know how to act in this world, we can find out by discovering how God
acted in this world—and this passage tells us.

He wasn't, and isn't, a God who hangs on to his dignity and high posi-
tion and refuses to let it go. Our God abandons his glory and comes down
to us just where we are. The servant king, born in a stable in Bethlehem.
A friend of publicans and sinners—the outcasts of society. (I wonder who
he would be friendly with in our society?) Some of those outcasts were
prostitutes. Others were Jews who collected taxes for the occupying
Roman authorities from their brother Jews, who hated them for it. But the
God who became a man and a servant (and a Jew) loved them. So much
that he died for them (and for us) by hanging on a cross. The glory of God
shone out of him when he was a man in our world and he said that he was
the light of the world. It shone out brightest of all from the cross, where
he was obedient to death—and to God.

A way to pray

Spend some time reflecting on the nature of God—made known in Jesus Christ.
Think of God—our creator, our servant and our lover. Christ died for love of us—to
suffer for our sins and to bring us to the Father. Think of the glory of God that shone
out of Jesus and showed us what God is like. Then confess, out loud (if you believe it)
that 'Jesus Christ is Lord'.

The body of Christ

It was not on tales artfully spun that we relied when we told you of the power of our Lord Jesus Christ and his coming; we saw him with our own eyes in majesty, when at the hands of God the Father he was invested with honour and glory, and there came to him from the sublime Presence a voice which said: 'This is my Son, my Beloved, on whom my favour rests.' This voice from heaven we ourselves heard; when it came, we were with him on the sacred mountain. All this only confirms for us the message of the prophets, to which you will do well to attend, because it is like a lamp shining in a murky place, until the day breaks and the morning star rises to illuminate your minds.

The glory of God is pretty daunting—unless he hides it. The tale that we are reading today (a true one, the writer tells us) is of a day when the glory of God shone out of Jesus and they saw it. It isn't that the writer is boasting. He is simply saying that this is what happened, and he is telling the truth. The disciples on the mount of transfiguration heard a voice from the Presence saying just who Jesus was. It confirmed the message of the prophets for them, and if their readers will also listen to it it will be a light for them in their darkness.

Before the transfiguration the disciples saw the man Jesus. Then, in the dazzling event, they saw Elijah the prophet and Moses the law-giver talking with Jesus. Afterwards they just saw Jesus. Perhaps as we read the Old Testament, or listen to it read in church, we can pray for the insight that connects the law and the prophets with Jesus, and with us. And when we are given the bread, in the service that is about communion between God and man through Christ, perhaps we can pray to be made aware of the glory of what is given to us: 'The body of Christ...'

Then the main crop

...For as all die in Adam, so all will be made alive in Christ. But each in his own order: Christ the first fruits, then at his coming those who belong to Christ. Then comes the end, when he hands over the kingdom to God the Father, after he has destroyed every ruler and every authority and power. For he must reign until he has put all his enemies under his feet. The last enemy to be destroyed is death. For 'God has put all things in subjection under his feet.' But when it says, 'All things are put in subjection,' it is plain that this does not include the one who put all things in subjection under him. When all things are subjected to him, then the Son himself will also be subjected to the one who put all things in subjection under him, so that God may be all in all.

If you have ever grown your own potatoes you will know what a special feeling it is to dig up the first plant when it is ready and boil the first new potatoes of the season. There will be others in the crop, like the first ones. And because we know what the 'first fruits' are like we know what the rest will be like. The Israelites always gave the first pickings to God, in an offering to the priests, as a sign that everything came from God and belonged to God.

The whole human race is 'in Adam', which means that we are all sinful and all mortal. We live for a few years and then die. It happens to all of us, but to all who are in Christ it is a different story. All who are in Christ are made alive with eternal life, a relationship with God the Father that begins in this life and goes on for ever in the next one. Living a life in which 'there will be no more death' (Revelation 21:4).

A reflection

Think of the first new potatoes being dug out of the ground, then think of the main crop. Think of the resurrection of Christ. Then think of the resurrection of all who are in Christ. Then be quiet for a few more moments, and let the wonder of this creation speak to you about the wonder of the new one that will be there on the other side of the grave.

Keep going; keep the word

A long time afterward, when the Lord had given rest to Israel from all their enemies all around... Joshua summoned all Israel... and said to them, 'I am now old and well advanced in years; and you have seen all that the Lord your God has done to all these nations for your sake, for it is the Lord your God who has fought for you. I have allotted to you as an inheritance for your tribes those nations that remain, along with all the nations that I have already cut off, from the Jordan to the Great Sea in the west. The Lord your God will push them back before you, and drive them out of your sight; and you shall possess their land, as the Lord your God promised you. Therefore be very steadfast to observe and do all that is written in the book of the law of Moses, turning aside from it neither to the right nor to the left.

Joshua was getting to the end of his life here on earth, but the Israelites hadn't got to the end of the task that God had called them to do. To possess the land of all the nations he had promised to give them—and to drive out the evil powers and rulers who were now in possession. They had started—but they hadn't finished. And we can start a new project with a big bang of enthusiastic energy which we can't keep going. So we settle down to enjoy our limited achievements and forget about those high hopes that we started with.

Not so God. The energy from his big bang is still sustaining the stars spinning in space and warming the worlds with its suns—all flowing from the creative word that God spoke in the darkness when he made the worlds and all the creatures who exist, including us. God created the world through his Word—and he holds it in being through the Word who is Christ. And for us who live in our world, in our generation—as for Joshua and the people of God in theirs—the way to possess the nations for God is through the living Word and the written word—that speaks of justice and righteousness and holiness, and tells us of the love of God for his world.

Try to remember

What did you mean to do for God when you started?

The water of life

Then he showed me the river of the water of life, bright as crystal, flowing from the throne of God and of the Lamb through the middle of the street of the city; also, on either side of the river, the tree of life with its twelve kinds of fruit, yielding its fruit each month; and the leaves of the tree were for the healing of the nations. There shall no more be anything accursed, but the throne of God and of the Lamb shall be in it, and his servants shall worship him; they shall see his face, and his name shall be on their foreheads. And night shall be no more; they need no light of lamp or sun, for the Lord God will be their light, and they shall reign for ever and ever.

Yesterday morning I arranged a bowl of honeysuckle, and the lovely pink and yellow flowers and green leaves on their twining stems hung over the edge of the vase. But in the evening some of the flowers and leaves had gone limp, and I saw that they were out of water. So I plunged them deep into a bowl of cold water—and this morning they have revived. No living thing can survive without water. Our bodies are 80 per cent water—and without ordinary water our bodies die. But there is a more serious death than the death of our bodies, and without the water of life our souls die. Our soul is our true self—the person God created us to be—and we can only be our true self in a relationship with God.

When he spoke to the thirsty Samaritan woman at the well Jesus said, 'If you knew the gift of God, and who it is that is saying to you "Give me a drink" you would have asked him and he would have given you living water.' If we drink that water it becomes in us 'a spring of water welling up to eternal life'. The river that flows from the throne of God is like the river that Ezekiel saw in his vision in the temple—and the river of life flows out of the place in the temple where the sacrifices were made.

A way to pray

Imagine the river that flows from the throne of God. Sit by it, and swim in it, and pray.

Daily Bible reading notes from BRF

If you have enjoyed reading and using *Day by Day with Shelagh Brown* you may wish to know that similar material is available from BRF in a regular series of Bible reading notes. *New Daylight* is published three times a year, in January, May and September, and contains a Bible reading, comment and prayer or meditation for every day. It also contains The BRF Magazine which has details of BRF events, developments, news and resources, as well as articles on the Christian life, the Bible, prayer and spirituality. *New Daylight* is also available in a large print edition.

New Daylight is available from your local Christian bookshop or, in case of difficulty, direct from BRF.